NEW PAYMENT WORLD

New Payment World

A Manager's Guide to Creating an Efficient Payment Process

Mary S. Schaeffer

John Wiley & Sons, Inc.

This book is printed on acid-free paper.♾

Published by John Wiley & Sons, Inc., Hoboken, New Jersey.
Published simultaneously in Canada.

Wiley Bicentennial Logo: Richard J. Pacifico

For general information on our other products and services, or technical support, please contact our Customer Care Department within the United States at 800-762-2974, outside the United States at 317-572-3993 or fax 317-572-4002.

Wiley also publishes its books in a variety of electronic formats. Some content that appears in print may not be available in electronic books.

For more information about Wiley products, visit our Web site at http://www.wiley.com.

Library of Congress Cataloging-in-Publication Data:

Schaeffer, Mary S.
New payment world : a manager's guide to creating an efficient payment process / Mary S. Schaeffer.
p. cm.
Includes bibliographical references and index.
ISBN 978-0-470-12054-5 (cloth)
1. Electronic funds transfers. 2. Payment. 3. Checks. 4. Clearinghouses. 5. Check fraud. I. Title.
HG1710.S33 2007
658.15′5—dc22

2007002355

Printed in the United States of America.

10 9 8 7 6 5 4 3 2 1

For Ben and Lara Ludwig,
two forward-thinking individuals who have
greatly enriched my life.

CONTENTS

PREFACE

This is a book about a revolution that quietly began a few years ago. It is about change in a function that you may not have given much thought to: your payment function. It may not be very different today from what it was 5 or 10 years ago. But here's a guarantee: It will be very different 5 or 10 years from now. And best of all, it will cost less!

Ten years ago you may not have been as concerned about escalating costs, check fraud, inefficient processes, demands from vendors, and headcount reductions as you are today. Even if you were, the cost-efficient payment alternatives currently available were just not to be had. Extremely low-cost electronic payment vehicles, corporate procurement cards, and even lower-cost wire transfers are all making an impact on the number of paper checks percolating through the system.

The book begins with an overview of how organizations of all types are paying their bills today. It contains the results of several surveys, which forecast how the business leaders believe they will be paying invoices five years from now. If you think paper checks are the way to go, these data will be a real eye-opener. And, yes, currently paper checks are used for the majority of all corporate payments.

This analysis is followed by a long list of problems caused by the paper check. In case you have not already surmised, the villain in this book is the paper check. Not only are the problems numerous, but the costs associated with the check, especially when compared to ACH payments and corporate procurement cards, are prohibitive. Often, unless time is taken to reflect on the problems as a whole, few realize what a huge burden paper checks have turned into.

Before moving on to investigate the payment tools currently available, Part One, "Payment Overview," investigates international payments and letters of credit. Letters of credit are included in this Part as they are used extensively in the international arena.

The book moves on to an in-depth analysis of each of the payment tools currently used for payment purposes (Part Two). Specifically, it dissects paper checks, wire transfers and electronic data interchange (EDI), p-cards, other cards, e-payments (both debits and credits), and then looks at some of the other payment products on the market today. These tend to be created by financial institutions as well as some third-party developers.

Chapter 9, "Other Payment Initiatives," also discusses the much-maligned petty cash box. It offers a breakdown of the features that are frequently included in the integrated payment initiatives coming to market and also analyzes some of the procure-to-pay initiatives.

Part Three then takes a very practical turn, offering advice to those either starting or expanding p-card or e-payment programs. It also includes a chapter that discusses how an organization can set up an integrated payment program that uses all the different payment tools currently available.

The payment world is not without outsourcing solutions. In fact, I believe that many of the products on the market mirror the services of some of the new electronic products available. Sometimes the line between a third-party product offering and the actual outsourcing is hard to tell. In fact, more than occasionally the line has become so blurred that it is hard to tell the difference, other than the name. This issue is discussed extensively in Chapter 15, "Outsourcing," along with the implications of these trends both for the organization and the individual professional. Advice is offered for the professional concerned about these trends.

Chapters 16 and 17 focus on fraud. Chapter 16 addresses the ongoing fight against check fraud along with recommendations on how to fight it in your own organization. Changes in the Uniform

Commercial Code (UCC) now make it imperative that organizations employ certain controls, or they will be held liable for the fraud that occurs on their watch.

Finally, Chapter 17 provides a discussion of fraud in the ACH world. While it not nearly as prevalent as in the check world, it does exist, and it is only a matter of time before it grows. A word of caution to those who are not currently making ACH payments: Do not overlook this chapter. Just because you are not making ACH payments does not mean some fraudster won't try to steal your money via ACH fraud. Everyone needs to take precautions, and they are discussed in this chapter.

Chapter 18 contains some concluding remarks as well as a list of recommendations to make your payment process more efficient.

The payment process for your organization will be radically different five years from now from what it is today, even if you have already made some radical changes. While I don't believe we are getting close to a paperless payment system, the rebellion against checks has definitely started. This book will provide you with the information you need to make sure your organization doesn't get left behind in the payment revolution that has already started. I wish you the best of luck.

MARY SCHAEFFER
June 2007

PART ONE

PAYMENT OVERVIEW

This part provides the background information related to the payment function today. Through the use of information gleaned from several surveys, it presents a picture of what the payment arena looks like today and what it will look like in five years. This background sets the stage for the rest of the book.

Since most organizations still rely heavily on checks to make payments, we dissect the payment process, identifying all the problems associated with a check-based payment system. And, as you are probably ever so painfully aware, there are many problems. With this foundation laid, it becomes clearer than ever as to why alternatives to the paper check are now so attractive.

Also addressed are international payment initiatives as well as letters of credit. Although they are used in domestic transactions, they are heavily relied on in the international marketplace.

1

Payment Arena Yesterday, Today, and Tomorrow

INTRODUCTION

The payment process in the business world, for both corporates and not-for-profits, is undergoing a quiet evolution. Techniques that were used by only a few organizations considered to be on the bleeding edge just a few short years ago are becoming commonplace. Interestingly, these techniques have not been limited to a few big companies with money to spend on the newest technologies. There has been widespread adoption, across industry and size lines. What's more, looking forward, organizations of all sorts expect to emulate the success of the payment pioneers who blazed the trail.

Part of the reason for the widespread adoption of new technologies is the low cost. In fact, in many instances, adoption of these technologies will result in lower costs, something that no organization can afford to ignore. Additionally, unlike some of the precursors (think electronic data interchange [EDI]), the new payment methodologies are easy to understand and often have their roots in the consumer world. Thus, when executives are first presented with proposals to take the new route, they understand what is being put before them. Combine the ease of understanding with the cost savings and often improved internal controls, and it is easy to understand why this payment revolution is taking place.

PAYMENT WORLD YESTERDAY

It wasn't too long ago that companies paid all their bills with checks and perhaps a few wire transfers for large-dollar items or funds going overseas. Checks were routinely signed by hand, with two signatures being required for most. The paper-heavy process was cumbersome and laden with problems.

A small number of large companies used financial EDI, the electronic movement of payments and payment-related information through the banking system in a standard format between two parties. EDI, with its rigid standards, worked because the standards were developed and everyone using the same "definition" meant the same thing. Although the EDI process was and is cumbersome, it allowed for some automation of the payment process. It is still around today mainly because of the large investment some companies have made in their systems.

While check forgery has always been a problem, it was not until the 1970s and 1980s that the fraud became a serious issue across the board. Prior to changes in the Uniform Commercial Code (UCC) in the early 1990s, banks routinely absorbed all the losses associated with check fraud. Thus there was little incentive for organizations to take safeguards in order to limit the losses.

With the changes in the UCC and the shared responsibility came new products to minimize check fraud as well as the emerging acceptance of electronic payment methodology. While direct deposit of payroll and Social Security payments have been around for many years, for the most part, that was the extent of electronic payments in the United States.

The United States might be a world leader in many arenas, but when it came to electronic payments, it was definitely a laggard. Interestingly, despite the efforts of many financial institutions to move their clients to electronic payment methodology, the impetus came from the consumer side. Some of this credit has to go to eBay and PayPal. As consumers became comfortable with online auctions and paying for the goods online, they became less reluctant to pay their own bills electronically.

At the same time, banks everywhere were touting the benefits of their online bill payment services. First with their mortgage and insurance payments, consumers started to make the move. For most, once they tried it, they found they liked it. This consumer acceptance led executives who had tried it at home to be more amenable to electronic payment methodology at work. Thus, these consumer movements have set the stage for the advances we are today experiencing in the payment arena.

PAYMENT WORLD TODAY

Today, organizations have a wide variety of payment methodologies available to them. Checks, while still accounting for the largest number of payments, are no longer King of the Hill. Over 87% of all companies now make some sort of automated clearinghouse (ACH) payments. This is just one of the nuggets of information *Accounts Payable Now & Tomorrow* mined from the study it conducted called, "The Future of Accounts Payable." One of the issues it looked at was how companies are making payments today as well as where they saw their payment structures going five years down the road.

Initiating Check Payments

Accounts payable initiates the lion's share of check payments. The data show that in only a few organizations are checks done outside accounts payable. We suspect that these isolated instances are checkbooks given to remote locations for emergency use. While there may be a business requirement necessitating check issuance outside of accounts payable, such a practice is not recommended as it tends to open the door to fraud and/or duplicate payments. Organizations that feel they must have the ability to issue a check outside accounts payable should insist on tight internal controls.

Outsourcing is still not a huge factor in accounts payable. In just 2% of the cases, check payments are outsourced. To see how your check payment practices stack up, review the payment data from the study shown in Exhibit 1.1.

ACH: Electronic Payments for Everyone

In the past, the only way to make an electronic payment was via wire transfers, which tend to be costly. Now, thanks to the ACH, the cost factor has disappeared. In fact, most studies show that paying with an ACH is significantly cheaper than paying with a paper check. There has been a lot of talk and haranguing about ACH. The data from the survey discussed earlier was an eye opener. Just under 90% of the respondents report making ACH payments. This is heartening because once an organization pays one or two vendors via the ACH (also called direct payment), it is likely to increase that activity.

While over half the ACH payments are initiated in accounts payable, a good portion are not. This can lead to duplicate payment trouble if appropriate controls are not put in place. Vendors should be designated as being paid either with a check, ACH, or purchase card (p-card). Only one payment vehicle should be used for each vendor. This is a relatively new concern but one all organizations need to address.

Making Check Payments	
Accounts payable department:	92.39%
Partially in AP, partially elsewhere:	2.17%
Other department:	3.26%
Outsourced:	2.17%
Don't know, N/A at our company:	0 0.00%
Making ACH Payments	
Accounts payable department:	51.61%
Partially in AP, partially elsewhere:	23.66%
Other department:	11.83%
Outsourced:	0 0.00%
Don't know, N/A at our company:	12.90%
Wire Transfers	
Accounts payable department:	29.67%
Partially in AP, partially elsewhere:	30.77%
Other department:	34.07%
Outsourced:	0.00%
Don't know, N/A at our company:	5.49%

EXHIBIT 1.1 WHO MAKES PAYMENTS FOR CORPORATE AMERICA

Source: *Accounts Payable Now & Tomorrow*, "Future of AP Survey 2007."

U.S. consumers use the ACH network primarily to pay bills automatically and electronically, and to receive income and benefit payments via direct deposit. National Automated Clearing House Association (NACHA) estimates that 6.5 to 7.0 billion consumer bills were collected via the ACH network in 2005, including preauthorized debits, Internet and telephone payments, and checks converted into ACH payments.

In the past, whenever the topic of financial EDI was raised, many executives' eyes would start to glaze over. It wasn't an interesting subject, and in many ways it was alien to everything they understood. Its proponents didn't help themselves by talking about things like ANSI X12 standards and 810 and 820 transaction sets. ACH methodology isn't hampered by such an albatross. Because of their consumer experiences, as discussed, most managers are comfortable with the idea of electronic payments.

Wire Transfer Payments

While accounts payable initiates most check payments, responsibility for other types of payments are shared or handled in other areas, primarily treasury. This is especially true when it comes to wire transfers. As you can see from Exhibit 1.1, accounts payable is not necessarily in control when it comes to wire transfer payments. This can lead to trouble if records are not updated accurately and quickly.

What does this mean? Consider this not-uncommon scenario. For whatever reason, payment to a key supplier was not made. The supplier is refusing to take any additional orders until it receives payment. The supplier may be unreasonable, or it may know it has your company between a rock and a hard place so it insists on a wire transfer. Because your company needs the supplier, it acquiesces. Wires of this sort are often handled in the treasury department. Once the payment is made, everyone breathes a sigh of relief because your organization will get whatever it needed so desperately from this supplier.

What often gets forgotten in this process, however, is updating the accounting records (i.e., make sure the purchase order [PO] is closed and the receiving records adjusted accordingly). If this is not done, when that missing invoice eventually surfaces—and they always do—it will be processed through normal channels. Now the only thing preventing a duplicate payment is someone's memory, and that is not a good control. In fact, depending on someone's memory is almost a guarantee of a duplicate payment.

Therefore, special controls should be put in place when payments are made by wire. Part of that process should be a requirement to update records when a rush wire is made. Since these are often made outside of accounts payable, we sometimes forget that rush wires can be just as disruptive as rush checks. Making the matter even worse, rush wires tend to be for higher-dollar amounts. And almost all organizations make some wire transfers. The data in the *Accounts Payable Now & Tomorrow* survey shows that only 5.49% of responding organizations don't do wire transfers.

P-Cards

P-cards, also referred to as purchasing cards, corporate procurement cards, and purchase cards, have become the payment vehicle of choice for many when it comes to small-dollar items. The definition of what's small varies from organization to organization. For some it's under $100, and others it's under $5,000. A few organizations put no dollar limit on the purchases that can be put on their p-card.

Initially, some organizations were concerned that their employees would take the cards and make all sorts of unauthorized purchases on them. Has that happened? Yes, but only in limited circumstances. Most card programs require that employees sign a document stating that they understand that they can be fired immediately if the card is used inappropriately. And in a few instances, companies had to let employees go because the cards were used in ways that did not benefit the company. However, these instances have been few and far between.

Very gradually, companies that feared these programs are starting to accept them, and managers who were reluctant to give their employees the cards are getting over those fears.

Routinely, even after they've been in corporate use for well over a decade, some vendors will send an invoice even though the item was paid for with a corporate p-card. This has created new challenges for those trying to avoid duplicate payments. And it probably foreshadows a similar problem with payments made through the ACH. This doesn't mean that the payment methodology should not be used; it simply shows the necessity for developing monitoring and control routines to ensure the duplicate payment does not occur because of the different payment methodologies.

Concluding Thoughts on Payment Methodology

The payment world is changing. There is widespread acceptance of the ACH as a payment vehicle. The survey also revealed that while checks are almost always initiated in accounts payable, other payment vehicles are not. This means that the corporate world will need to change the processes and controls that surround payments to ensure that the appropriate records are updated in a very timely manner. Otherwise it will quickly find itself plagued with fraud and duplicate payments. This is an opportunity for accounts payable to take the lead and force the discussion on these issues and insist that strong internal controls be instituted to protect the organization—which will show that accounts payable is about more than just paying bills!

PAYMENT WORLD TOMORROW

It doesn't take a genius to predict that for most organizations, the way they pay their bills will change in the next five years. We fully expect the number of paper checks to decrease and the number of electronic payments to increase. Paper checks will take a further hit at those organizations using p-cards. Two recent studies back these assertions.

As part of the *Accounts Payable Now & Tomorrow* survey, respondents indicated that although only 34% were making payments using ACH five years ago, five years from now, 91% expect to be doing so. Clearly not only will the use of ACH expand to a greater number of organizations, but those using it will find ways to expand existing usage.

The 2005 Palmer and Gupta Purchasing Card Benchmark Survey revealed that the p-card approach is moving to smaller organizations as the concept becomes more widely accepted. Additionally, most organizations using p-cards are increasing their spend on their cards. The study forecast per annum growth over the next few years in the average of 10 to 15%. Thus, we can expect p-cards to remain a viable part of the payment structure for many years to come.

While we do not expect to see the complete demise of the paper check anytime soon, we do expect to see their use continue to diminish in the corporate world. Their place will be taken by electronic payments and use of p-cards. Additionally, and this will be discussed in more detail in Chapter 8 on e-payments, very gradually organizations will allow certain select parties to debit their accounts for monies owed. While this is commonly done in other countries, the United States will continue to be a laggard in this payment methodology. Some companies now use this approach to pay sales tax and in situations where they are captive to a certain vendor. An example of this might be a service station that pays for deliveries of gas and other supplies.

The changing payment paradigm may result in closer integration between the accounts payable function and the treasury function, if treasury is taking the lead with electronic payments. How the staffing function plays out remains to be seen, although initial indications are that it will not be as it was in the past.

AN EMERGING ISSUE: PAYMENT CONTROL

As part of the above mentioned survey, readers were asked who made the various types of payments within their organization. The results are shown in Exhibit 1.1. While typically checks are drawn in accounts payable, when it comes to initiating other types of payments, the responsibility is not located in one department. Accounts payable retains control of the payment process only slightly more than half the time when ACH payments are used and even less when wire transfers are the mode of payment.

The increased number of hands in the payment pie means that a duplicate payment is more likely to occur. As we saw with the introduction of p-cards into the corporate payment arena, vendors are not always able to adjust their processes to accommodate the needs of their customers using the new technology. Hence it is imperative that the organizations using differing payment approaches take care to ensure that controls are in place that will not permit duplicate payments. This issue will be discussed in greater detail in Chapter 14 on integrating your program.

2

Payment Problems and Issues Facing the Corporate World

INTRODUCTION

The payment world has gotten a lot more complicated. A variety of far-reaching issues have affected the process. These issues were often the impetus for the change that generated the new payment vehicles and processes discussed in this book. An understanding of the issues and the implications of those problems will help readers craft their ultimate payment process. It should also help them understand the demands of their banks and their payment processing professionals.

FLOAT

In the days of double-digit interest rates and sometimes lengthy mail delays, a focus on float was realistic. Use of remote disbursement points added to the "benefit." Improved mail times and lower interest rates make the savings that can be attributable to float far less significant. What's worse, as companies stretch payments in an attempt to gain a slight financial advantage, they run the risk of antagonizing much-needed suppliers.

Still, float remains an issue when use of electronic payments enters the fray. Float reflects the added benefit organizations experience due to the time it takes a check to clear the bank. Typically it is measured in days. Should it turn out to be an obstacle in your plans for an improved payment program, try this three-step approach:

Step 1. Calculate the financial gain your organization gets from float. Is that a significant figure, or are you wasting a lot of time for just a few dollars?

Step 2. If the figure is an amount that your organization takes seriously, figure out what it costs you to get it. For example, calculate your check costs compared to your costs of issuing an electronic payment. Do the costs outweigh the benefits?

Step 3. If you think float is an issue, go to your vendors and try to renegotiate the payment terms to make the transaction float neutral to both parties.

Don't overlook the recent (March 16, 2007) changes in the back office clearing processes for checks under $25,000. This change effectively removes the processing float associated with these checks.

EARLY PAYMENT DISCOUNTS

As organizations everywhere look for ways to enhance their bottom line and interest rates on low-risk investments continue to hover in the mid-single-digit area, early payment discounts have become a very hot issue. In fact, one manager says that the only "mortal sin" in her payment area is missing an early payment discount. The reason for this is quite simple. Early payment discounts translate into an annual rate of return of 36%, for 2/10 net 30 terms.

Some vendors offer this financial incentive to entice their customers to pay early. The most common enticement is the 2/10 net 30 payment terms. As most reading this are well aware, this means that although the payment is due on the 30th day, customers can take a 2% discount if paying before the 10th day. Any introductory finance book will walk you through the math that demonstrates that 2/10 net 30 is equivalent to a 36% rate of return; hence even 1/10 net 30 translates into an 18% rate of return.

While the individual amounts may seem small, they do add up. Losing a 2% discount on a $10,000 invoice may only result in $200 not earned, but multiply that by the number of invoices processed and the amounts start to add up.

This issue becomes even more crucial for companies operating on razor-thin margins, as this extra return can make a huge difference in the bottom line. Yet many organizations have such cumbersome and inefficient processes that it is impossible to get the invoice turned around in the requisite 10 days. This is especially true when paper invoices are mailed and have to be approved before a payment can be made. The more paper-intensive a process is, the less likely an organization is to be able to get through the process in time to earn the discount.

This is one of the drivers for organizations to move to both electronic payments and electronic invoicing. In the past, some vendors were willing to look the other way when a payment where the discount was taken was received a few days late; most are no longer so accommodating. In the current interest rate environment, many vendors are looking for any excuse to get away from offering early payment discounts. As attractive as the discount may be to the recipient, it is equally unattractive to those offering it.

PAYMENT TERMS: THEIRS, OURS, AND REALITY

Ideally the terms are spelled out in the contract and purchase order. Under the best of circumstances, the terms are agreed to during the contract negotiations or are stated when the purchase order (PO) is provided. However, when it comes to payment terms, best practices and reality are often on two different planes.

Often organizations will set payment terms across the board with little regard to what their suppliers' offered payment terms are. Whose terms prevail under these conditions often depends on who is the 800-pound gorilla in the relationship. Generally the terms of the organization that needs the other the most will prevail.

That's not the worst thing that can cause friction when it comes to payment terms. Some companies will decide that they will pay in 45 or 60 days and never tell their vendors. They simply start paying late. Most who take this approach, and these organizations are not in the majority, never reveal this when the contract is signed or the order placed. This type of behavior leads to strained vendor relations and wastes time and person power in accounts payable when vendors call looking for their funds shortly after they were due.

It is generally recommended that if your payment terms are anything other than the norm, you inform vendors of them. Occasionally, stretched payment terms are a financial necessity for organizations going through tough financial times. It's much better for the long-term relationship to explain the situation and ask for vendor understanding than to pay late and hope for the best.

SUPPLIER DEMANDS REGARDING PAYMENT TOOLS

Sometimes vendors who are in the driver's seat get picky about how they want to be paid. Even if you've decided that you will stick with paper checks for your payment process, you may find yourself forced to reevaluate that stance. Recognizing the benefits of both purchase cards (p-cards) and electronic payments, some vendors are demanding that their customers use one or the other of these payment vehicles if they want to continue doing business with the supplier.

Thus, the company that thought it could avoid being thrust into the new payment revolution may unexpectedly find itself right in the middle of it. Don't despair if this happens. An interesting scenario often unfolds in such cases. The organization that had to be dragged kicking and screaming into the new payment world finds, after trying it, that it likes the new approach. When that happens, the organization inevitably turns into a missionary convincing other suppliers to take payment in the same manner.

What may have started out as a supplier requirement sometimes turns into a customer demand. After experiencing the benefits, many organizations turn to their other suppliers asking that they accept payment in the same manner.

COST OF PRODUCING A CHECK

There's no fancy way to say this: Even in the most efficient organizations, checks are expensive to produce—and they cause a lot of problems. While automated clearinghouse (ACH) items are generally estimated to cost 10 cents apiece and p-card payments usually result in a rebate to the company, checks are estimated to cost anywhere from $3 to $20+, depending on the processes used to create the payment.

You don't have to do too much math to figure out that it doesn't make a lot of sense to use a check to pay for a $2 widget or, for that matter, even a $50 or $100 expenditure. Common sense and the cost and processing efficiencies associated with p-cards and ACH are driving the move from paper checks.

DUPLICATE PAYMENTS

Duplicate payments are a dirty little secret in the business world that few like to discuss in public. But they are a fact of corporate life. In a recent *Accounts Payable Now & Tomorrow* survey, accounts payable professionals were asked if within the last three years they had ever had a supplier return a check indicating it was a duplicate. Just under 95% indicated they had. To be exact, 94.92% said they'd had a check returned by an honest vendor. Now, as most reading this are ever-so-painfully aware, few vendors will actually return the duplicate payment. Most deposit it and hope you never figure it out.

To determine if the increased awareness of the problem has made organizations more careful, respondents were asked about changes in the number of duplicates. Keep in mind something about duplicate payments. Like fraud, people can only report on the duplicates that they know about. If duplicate payments have been made but not identified, the assumption is they don't exist. And there is sometimes a reticence to admit mistakes, although given the 95% figure just cited, this discretion appears to have all but disappeared.

Survey respondents were asked if they thought the number of duplicate payments at their organization had decreased as compared with three years ago. Slightly more than half (50.85%) said they thought the number had declined. Don't assume that the other half reported making a larger number of duplicate payments; that is not the case. Over one-third (37.29%) indicated that they simply did not know whether the number of duplicates had increased at their organization. Only about 12% thought they had increased.

As organizations have been using multiple payment initiatives, often initiated in multiple departments, it is crucial that the appropriate controls be built into the process to ensure that duplicate payments don't increase.

SARBANES-OXLEY AND INTERNAL CONTROLS

With the passage of the Sarbanes-Oxley Act in 2002 and its requirements, public companies were forced to take a look at their internal controls surrounding all procedures, including their payment process. The requirement that management certify that appropriate controls were in place certainly got them to pay attention in those few organizations where controls in accounts payable were not considered to be a big deal.

The passage of the act had an interesting side effect. Even organizations not required to conform to the strictures of the act were found to have taken a second look at their processes. It appears that the activities that led to the Sarbanes-Oxley requirements served as a wake-up call to many companies that were not required by law to change. In an *Accounts Payable Now & Tomorrow* survey, participants were asked about changes made in their organization as a result of Sarbanes-Oxley.

While only 30% of the respondents were public companies, 57% admitted changing their travel and entertainment policies and 43% said it was key in getting support for strengthened backup requirements for check requests. Lesser numbers of respondents believed the act was critical in getting support for other internal control initiatives they wanted and were ultimately successful in implementing.

CHECK 21 AND ITS IMPACT

The Check Clearing for the 21st Century Act (Check 21) became effective on October 28, 2004. It was designed to foster innovation in the payments system and to enhance its efficiency by reducing some of the legal impediments to check truncation. Truncation is the conversion of a check to an electronic debit or image of the check, which serves as the official record.

The net result is that checks clear faster. Without going through the legal and banking fine print, Check 21 allows checks to be converted to electronic items that pass through the system faster. In theory, this would help thwart check fraud.

Thus, once again the groundwork was being laid for organizations to become familiar with electronic transactions. While by itself Check 21 certainly didn't lead to the elimination of paper checks, it is one more factor that helped executives become comfortable with a payment structure that did not revolve around paper.

CORPORATE COST-CUTTING INITIATIVES

As organizations continue to be pushed on the profitability front, executives continue to look everywhere to cut costs and headcount. As mentioned earlier in this chapter, paper checks are an expensive way for an organization to pay its bills. Thus the cost savings associated with both ACH payments and p-cards made both vehicles very attractive. And that is just the beginning.

Headcount has become a serious issue. As the number of organizations requiring across-the-board headcount reductions grows, the payment function has come under attack. Because of its very nature, a paper-intensive process is also people intensive. As accounts payable departments are forced to cut headcount, they have to find a way to handle the same or greater volume with fewer people. Inevitably that means moving away from paper checks to p-cards and ACH, both of which generally require a smaller staff.

When the cost savings are combined with the headcount reductions that often occur with payment vehicles other than paper checks, the move becomes irresistible.

CHANGES IN UCC

By the early 1990s, check fraud had become a thriving business. The losses associated with it had become intolerable, and banks, which had once absorbed the losses to maintain good customer relations, were beginning to revolt. To be honest, they had good reason. By employing lax procedures when it came to their checks, many companies did not do enough to help stop the tidal wave of fraud. In the early 1990s, the Uniform Commercial Code (UCC) was changed to put the responsibility for the loss with the party best in a position to prevent it.

Articles 3 and 4 of the UCC describe the responsibilities needed under the concepts of ordinary care and comparative negligence. The losses associated with a particular fraud are allocated to the parties sharing the responsibility for the prevention of the check fraud. The distribution depends on each party's ability to prevent the fraud. In other words, it depends on the amount of contributory negligence each party is assessed.

The other factor in determining liability is a concept called ordinary care. Bank customers are required to follow "reasonable commercial standards" for their industry or business. This seemingly innocuous statement can have significant ramifications—so don't overlook it. An organization's failure to exercise ordinary care will be considered to have substantially contributed to the fraud. To put it another way, the organization is considered to have neglected its obligation to exercise ordinary care.

No longer can an organization look the other way. It must employ reasonable processes around its check handling. For many, one easy way around this is to minimize the number of checks written.

IMPACT OF CHECK AND EMPLOYEE FRAUD

The changes in the UCC just described helped put a stop to the growing losses associated with check fraud. However, from a corporate perspective, the changes in the UCC also shifted some of the potential losses from their banks to them. In fact, some on the corporate side do not consider the changes in the UCC a good thing. After all, before those modifications, they did not have to worry about check losses. With the changes in the UCC, organizations are responsible for some or all of the losses due to check fraud.

Additionally, employee fraud is a concern. Sometimes referred to as occupational fraud, it can be a serious issue. Every two years, in a widely awaited *Report to the Nation*, the Association of Certified Fraud Examiners (ACFE) provides an update on this topic.

ACFE describes occupational fraud as "the use of one's occupation for personal enrichment through the deliberate misuse or misapplication of the employing organization's resources or assets." Of those cases reported, 91.5% involve asset misappropriations with a median loss of $150,000, according to the 2006 report.

Check tampering is defined as "any scheme in which a person steals his or her employer's funds by forging or altering a check on one of the organization's bank accounts, or steals a check the organization has legitimately issued to another payee." This is done by the employee either stealing blank company checks, or taking a check made out to a vendor and depositing it into his or her own bank account. A little over 17% of the asset misappropriation frauds were related to check tampering, and there was a median loss of $120,000 associated with this type of fraud.

Long-term trusted employees continue to have a stranglehold on this type of crime. Larger losses are associated with employees in higher positions as well as those who have been employed for a longer time. There is a direct correlation between the size of the loss and these two factors.

Men are over one and a half times more likely than women to commit this type of fraud, and, when they do, the losses are two and a half times as large. This is likely tied to the fact that in most organizations, men tend to hold higher positions than women.

Executive/upper management account for over one-third of all this type of crime and accounting commits just under 32% of it. When it comes to check tampering, accounting (probably because of its familiarity with the issues) is responsible for a whopping 57.4% of the cases with executive/upper management responsible for another 26.4% of the cases.

3

International Payments and Letters of Credit

INTRODUCTION

Whether you do business internationally or not, at least occasionally most organizations have to make a payment in a foreign currency. This can present some headaches. There are some easy ways to take care of small one-time expenditures, but for more complex and ongoing transactions, payment can be a bit more problematical. If international trade is a big part of your organization's business, you will in all likelihood need to learn about letters of credit. And then, of course, there are the problems that inevitably arise due to differing currencies.

DIFFERENCES BETWEEN DOMESTIC AND INTERNATIONAL EXCHANGES

One of the things that many executives like best about international trade is that in other countries, longer payment terms are the norm. While the terms will vary from country to country and industry to industry, net 30 is not the default. Actual payment terms should be negotiated as part of the contract and given to the party responsible for making the payment.

While payment terms may be longer, cash in advance is also more common. Do not be surprised if at the beginning of a new relationship, the vendor asks for cash in advance of shipping the goods.

When it comes to paper checks, most of the rest of the world has left the United States in the dust. For day-to-day transactions, few use paper checks.

Many terms can be associated with the transaction reflecting who is required to pay for freight and insurance and when the title to the goods passes ownership. This is extremely important as it affects the ultimate cost as well as what the purchaser has to do—such as getting insurance. Again, this should be spelled out in the contract and reflected on the purchase order (PO) or pro-forma invoice.

INTERNATIONAL WIRES

When initiating an international wire, it is important that the instructions include a reference to which network you would like used. Otherwise, it is left to the discretion of the financial intermediary, and that can sometimes result in cost and process inefficiencies. Internationally, wires can be made via one of these networks:

- *SWIFT.* The Society for Worldwide Interbank Financial Telecommunication is the industry-owned cooperative supplying secure, standardized messaging services and interface software to nearly 8,000 financial institutions in 206 countries and territories. In recognition of falling technology prices and competition from other payment methodologies over the past 10 years, SWIFT message prices have been reduced over 80%.
- *CHIPS.* The Clearing House Interbank Payments System is a bank-owned payments system for clearing large-value

payments. CHIPS is a real-time, final payments system for U.S. dollars that uses bilateral and multilateral netting for maximum liquidity efficiency. CHIPS processes over 300,000 payments a day with a gross value of $1.5 trillion. This payments platform serves the largest banks from around the world, representing 19 countries.

If you are making transfers in U.S. dollars, the odds are high that you will use CHIPS. So your instructions should include the words "via CHIPS."

SMALL ONE-TIME EXPENDITURES

Occasionally you will find yourself with a small bill that requires payment in a foreign currency. If the purchase is small, say a subscription or conference attendance fee, a credit card will often do the trick. This is the ideal solution for those who do not regularly participate in the foreign exchange markets. Not only is this an easy solution, but you will get the best foreign exchange rate transacting this way as your order will get lumped into all the other transactions the card company is processing that day. And, as with other markets, there effectively are volume discounts.

It is recommended that even if the company doesn't have a company-sponsored credit card, the individual who is purchasing the item might be encouraged to use his or her own credit card and put in for compensation via the organization's Travel and Entertainment reimbursement process. If the credit card option is not available, you will in all likelihood have to call your bank and purchase a check in the requisite amount in the foreign currency. It will not be cheap.

CURRENCY ISSUES

Different nations have different monetary units, and the currency of one country rarely can be used for making payments in another country. The contract and PO should state what currency the goods are to be paid in.

If the contract calls for euros, do not take it upon yourself to convert that amount to U.S. dollars at the prevailing rate and send along the U.S. dollars. While most executives would not do this, it still occasionally happens and can cause trouble. In most cases the seller will not accept the payment—unless there has been a favorable move in the foreign exchange market. Then such payment might be accepted; still, it is not a good practice and will eventually lead to trouble.

LETTERS OF CREDIT

If used correctly, letters of credit are extremely useful in international trade. If you do any amount of business internationally, you will probably be asked to provide one at some point. Make sure that the letter of credit is filled out correctly and conforms to the business requirements. This may seem like trite advice, but incorrectly filled out letters of credit cause huge problems, and it happens all the time. Some experts estimate that 70% of all letters of credit have problems. Others think the number is higher!

Additionally, there must be adequate time on business side for the goods to be delivered, the necessary paperwork to be completed and delivered, and the documents to be presented to the bank. Sounds simple enough, but as anyone who has had anything to do with letters of credit knows only too well, "simple" is not a word one uses in conjunction with them.

Working Effectively with Letters of Credit

While letters of credit often fall under that old umbrella of "you can't live with them but you can't live without them," managers must find ways to use them effectively. Some innovative ways to use these exacting instruments are described next. While some techniques may appear to be deceptively simple, they are often overlooked.

- *Standardization.* With a one-size-fits-all approach, errors become less likely. Also, since fewer variances were allowed, the staff became more familiar with the fine nuances of their method. This policy also helps reduce errors since deviations are not permitted.
- *Get instructions from your vendors.* Ask for instructions on opening letters of credit along with an application for doing so. By addressing some of the fine points ahead of time, problems can be prevented before they could occur.

  While you may have gotten many letters of credit for other vendors, if it is a new relationship, there may be details that must be put in a letter of credit. It's quite possible that you will routinely put in something that does not match your documents. This doesn't make one party right and the other wrong, it just guarantees that the paperwork for the letters of credit won't agree and thus will be rejected by the bank.
- *Routing through one source.* By routing as many letters of credit as possible through your main bank and its foreign affiliates, you will be able to improve the consistency of presentations and payments. This helps minimize discrepancy fees. It also improves bank communications, which helps speed up payments.

  By focusing on as few banks as possible for your letter of credit activity, it is possible to speed things up. Ideally this activity will be limited to only one or two banks. The added volume will make you a valued customer, which should in turn lead to improved service when things go wrong. It also makes it easier on the staff who will then only have to learn how one or several banks do things. By limiting the number of banks' procedures that the staff must learn, you also limit the number of errors made.

Required Information

Letters of credit contain much information. In order that the document not be considered discrepant, every *t* needs to be crossed and all *i*'s dotted. Make sure that your letters of credit:

- Are irrevocable
- Are dated
- Specify the beneficiary and the account party
- Specify the amount
- Are numbered
- Are issued on bank stationery and signed
- Allow drafts at specific tenors to be drawn on the bank
- List the documents required

Bank Functions

While a rose by any other name may still smell sweet, a bank by another name will not still perform the same function when it comes to letters of credit. The number of different types of banks involved in letters of credit and their respective functions can be confusing, even for those with extensive international experience.

A list that defines the banks' roles in letter-of-credit transactions follows.

- *Issuing bank* initiates the letter of credit extending its guarantee to pay upon presentation of *proper* documentation.
- *Advising bank* is usually located in the beneficiary's country, which delivers the letter of credit to the beneficiary.
- *Confirming bank* is usually located in the beneficiary's country and adds its guarantee of payment. It can be the same as the advising bank, but it can also be another bank.
- *Negotiating bank* accepts documents for examination for payment.
- *Paying bank*, where drafts are drawn, is nominated to make payment. It is also sometimes referred to as the drawee.

- *Reimbursing bank* is where the issuing bank maintains balances to fund the paying/drawee bank's payment to the beneficiary.

UCP 500

It is most important for an international transaction that the letter of credit be subject to the Uniform Customs and Practices (UCP) for Documentary Credits. The latest version (published in May 1993 in both New York and Paris) is referred to as UCP 500. As those dealing in China have discovered, for example, the Bank of China is reluctant to include such a requirement. This has caused some concern in the credit community. Credit managers should be wary of any company that refuses to include the "subject to UCP 500" provision in a letter of credit.

The International Chamber of Commerce (ICC) views one of its core tasks as making it easier for companies in different countries to trade with each other. The means for achieving this include the ICC rules for the conduct of trade and payments. The UCP for Documentary Credits is one such set of rules.

The purpose of the 1993 revisions is to address new developments and technological applications. The revisions are also intended to improve the functionality of the rules. One of the complaints about UCP 400 was the number of discrepancies that appeared in documents allowing them to be rejected. It is not crystal clear if this problem is eliminated in this most recent revision. Still, UCP 500 provides a level playing field for international trade. At least all participants are playing with the same deck of cards. Or at least most are.

ISP98

As of January 1, 1999, standby letters of credit are governed for the first time by international agreement. The new rules in *International*

Standby Practices ISP98, issued by the Institute of International Banking Law and Practice, standardize the rules for using standby letters of credit worldwide and allow managers to negotiate standbys accurately, without being experts.

Once associated primarily with the U.S. market, the standby is now a fast-growing international product, exceeding commercial letters of credit in value terms by 5 to 1. In 1997, over $450 billion in standbys were held by non-U.S. banks in the U.S. market alone. The ISP98 rules reduce the cost and time of drafting, limit problems in handling, and avoid disputes and unnecessary litigation that resulted from the lack of internationally agreed-upon rules for standbys.

NEW STANDBY LETTERS OF CREDIT RULES

The new, internationally recognized ISP98 rules are to standby letters of credit what the UCP 500 has been to commercial credits. They contain definitions of key terms like "original" and "automatic amendment," cover the standby process from "obligations" to "syndication," and contain basic definitions should the standby involve electronic presentation of documents. Managers can obtain a copy of the *International Standby Practices ISP98* from International Chamber of Commerce Publishing (ICC Publishing, Inc., 156 Fifth Avenue, Suite 820, New York, NY 10010).

TYPES OF LETTERS OF CREDIT

Many professionals have learned the hard way that all letters of credit are not created equal. While most managers are familiar with the details of the basic letters of credit, there are six other types, each with its land mines waiting for the unwary: standby letters of credit, revolving letters of credit, deferred payment letters of credit, transferable letters of credit, back-to-back letters of credit, and, finally, red clause letters of credit. We will discuss standbys last as they have many uses and can be used to alleviate risk in rather different ways.

All are used primarily, but not exclusively, in international trade, where they facilitate the process of paying for goods sold in another country. But they can also be used to guarantee a transaction. In those instances, there is no intent to draw against the letter of credit unless the prearranged payment is not made.

Two other points must be made when considering any letters of credit. First, they should be confirmed in all instances, ideally, by a financially sound bank. Some professionals insist on a U.S. bank, but a reputable European or Asian bank is just as good.

Second, letters of credit should be irrevocable. If they are not, they are not worth the paper they are written on. After all, when is a bank likely to revoke the letters of credit? Only at the point where the financial situation of your buyer becomes so precarious that your payment is in danger—and that is the very point at which the protective features of the letters of credit are needed.

Revolving Letters of Credit

Revolving letters of credit typically are used in those instances where there is repeat business. By obtaining one letter of credit to handle multiple shipments, the administrative work with the bank is reduced. Limits can be placed on the amount and the timing of each draw. In these instances, it is intended that the letters of credit be drawn against. In order to do so, the seller presents the specified documents to the bank. Monitoring of such letters of credit is of vital importance, as a missed date can mean not getting paid on a timely basis.

Deferred Payment Letters of Credit

The deferred payment letter of credit is similar in many respects to a revolving one except that payment does not take place immediately. It is used in those cases where the seller agrees to offer extended terms to the buyer. With this type of letter of credit, the seller presents documents to the bank as soon as it receives them but does not receive payment until some agreed upon date in the future.

Besides the security feature, there is the advantage of having such a letter of credit over selling on open account. The seller can use the bank's promise of future payment to obtain credit from its own bank, effectively trading on the credit of the bank that issued the letter of credit.

The period of deferment usually exceeds six months, making this an attractive instrument in only a few cases—usually those involving heavy machinery or other goods where extended terms are more common.

Transferable Letters of Credit

When the seller of goods is actually only acting as a middleman, it may be necessary to have a letter of credit transferable in order to complete the transaction. Letters of credit typically are not transferable. However, it is possible to have the document marked as transferable. In this instance, the rights are passed on to the transferee (of which there can be more than one). All transferees must comply with the terms and conditions spelled out in the original letter of credit.

Usually, before any transfer is made, the beneficiary must send a request in writing to the bank to effect such a transfer. This is one more step in a process filled with paper and details. It also presents another opportunity for discrepancies to creep into the documents and another opening for banks to bounce those not properly completed, which will inevitably add time to the process. Those considering using transferable letters of credit should factor this fact into their time equation and make sure the letter of credit is issued for a long enough period to cover delays.

Many banks will not make these transfers until they have been paid for their services—another cause for delay. Most experts recommend that when transferable letters of credit are used, the dates should be prior to, and the amounts less than, the date and the amount of the original letter of credit.

Some experts refer to transferable letters of credit as assignable letters of credit. The two are the same. While the use of this type of letter of credit can often add complications to an already complex process, it is sometimes unavoidable.

Back-to-Back Letters of Credit

Back-to-back letters of credit are usually preferable to a transferable letter of credit—although banks are not generally thrilled with this type of an arrangement either. Again, it is often used by a middleman, typically one that might have trouble obtaining credit based on its own financials. With back-to-backs, the middleman asks a bank to issue a second letter of credit in favor of the ultimate supplier, using the letter of credit issued by the buyer as collateral for the second one.

In this arrangement, the terms and conditions of both letters of credit are identical except the amounts and dates in the second one must be smaller and earlier. The risk here is that the performance of the original letter of credit is contingent on the timely and perfect execution of the second. Those using such instruments are advised to be sure to leave plenty of time for delays.

Red Clause Letter of Credit

The red clause letter of credit is useful to those sellers who do not have adequate capital to produce (or purchase) goods that larger customers have ordered or would like to order. It permits the beneficiary to acquire an advance of all or part of the amount of the credit depending on the details spelled out in the letter of credit. Upon instructions from the buyer, the issuing bank authorizes the confirming bank to make a cash advance to the beneficiary.

The beneficiary (i.e., the seller) must provide a written guarantee against documents evidencing that shipment will be presented in compliance with the terms spelled out in the letter of credit. A close partnering arrangement between the buyer and the seller is usually necessary for this type of arrangement to work. It requires a financially strong buyer and a seller with a desirable product but limited financial resources. When production is complete, the seller presents final documents to the bank for payment. At that time, the bank will make payment less any funds advanced.

If the goods are not shipped, the paying bank looks to the issuing bank for reimbursement, not only of the funds advanced but interest charges as well. This amount is then charged to the buyer's account—regardless of whether the goods are ever received. It is obvious why this instrument is rarely used. However, it can be helpful in limited circumstances.

Standby Letters of Credit

Standby letters of credit are used most frequently to guarantee the performance or for services. They can be found backing bonds, loans, or future interest payments. They are put in place as a type of insurance with the intent that they never be drawn. However, if the underlying obligation is not met, the letter of credit can, and often is, drawn on by the beneficiary. The bank honoring the obligation will then either debit the bank account of the issuer or convert the obligation into a loan.

As with other types of letters of credit, in order to draw on it, the beneficiary must present documents to the bank. The exact documents needed, as with other letters of credit, are spelled out in the letter of credit itself. If this type of letter of credit is accepted by an exporter, it must be monitored just as all others to ensure that it does not expire before it is no longer needed. If it does expire, make sure to extend it—or draw on it if the other party refuses to cooperate.

Use of Standby Letter of Credit

Under a standby letter of credit, a bank promises to pay the exporter/ seller if its customer/buyer does not meet payment obligations as defined in the sales contract. The bank charges the buyer a fee for this. The Federal Reserve's board of governors (Regulation "H") defines standby letters of credit as:

> any letter of credit or similar arrangement, however named or described, which represents an obligation to the beneficiary on the part of the issuer:
>
> - To repay money borrowed by, advanced to or for the account of the account party;
> - To make payment on account of any indebtedness undertaken by the account party; or
> - To make payment on any default by the account party in the performance of an obligation.

With use of a standby letter of credit, both commercial documents and funds generally flow outside the letter of credit (between buyer and seller). The letter of credit is "standing by" for an event of default or nonperformance before it can be drawn on.

Special Purpose

The standby letter of credit is viewed by many as a special-purpose letter of credit. In such cases, the intent is that it will never be drawn but serves only as a "guarantee" of performance or payment. The commercial documents and the funds generally flow outside the letter of credit between the buyer and seller. The letters of credit are "standing by" for an event of default or nonperformance before they can be drawn on.

VAT

Value-added tax (VAT) is a consumer-oriented tax imposed on goods and services sold. As a taxable entity incurring VAT for business purposes, your organization may be entitled to a VAT refund in many European countries and Canada. To obtain a refund, an original invoice, together with an application form and other supporting documentation, must be submitted to the VAT authorities in the country where the expenditure was incurred. If this sounds simple, you've been deceived. It is anything but that.

Different countries have different rates, and VAT is recoverable on different items in different countries. Then there is the little issue of language. Most countries want invoices in their native language. It is a paper-intensive, heavily regulated, and deadline-ridden task. This is why it will probably come as no surprise to learn that most companies that reclaim VAT do so by outsourcing.

VAT can be a source of revenue for your organization, especially if you are not currently reclaiming VAT. While there are statutes of limitations, if you will, on how far back you can go, there is money to be had in your travel and expense files if your employees travel internationally and you are not currently reclaiming your VAT.

How far back can you go? Generally speaking, the limit is just one year. While this may be a bummer, it doesn't mean you shouldn't set your organization up so it can begin reclaiming in the future.

PAYMENT TREND

International trade is here to stay, and payment methodologies used to facilitate trade are crucial if your organization is to do business out of the country.

PART TWO

Payment Tools

The chapters in this part delve into the underpinnings of the payment tools that are currently in use in the business-to-business environment. Specifically, in this part we investigate:

- Paper checks
- Wire transfers
- Financial EDI
- P-cards
- Other cards
- ACH credits
- ACH debits
- Use of the petty cash box
- Other payment initiatives

These are the tools that will form the foundation of most, if not all, payment practices. It is imperative that you have a sound understanding of each in order to devise the best payment process for your organization.

4

Paper Checks

INTRODUCTION

Today the lion's share of payments in the corporate world in the United States are made by check. The portion of payments made by check is decreasing as other alternatives become more popular. Still, they are a big issue for most organizations. This chapter begins with a discussion of problems checks cause. As you go through this chapter, you will note that it seems to be filled with detailed minutia that you would prefer not to be bothered with. That is precisely the reason why so many professionals are trying to distance themselves and their organizations from paper checks.

CHECK PROBLEMS

Checks cause many organizations a lot of trouble. For starters, they are relatively expensive to produce. We're not only talking about the obvious expenses—the cost of purchasing checks and the postage used to mail them—but the salaries of your employees, who must spend their days producing, verifying, mailing, and reconciling checks as well as the myriad of other tasks related to the check production cycle.

The process of producing checks is people intensive. No matter how conscientious and hardworking they are, employees occasionally will introduce errors into the process. Errors add more costs to the process as it now takes more human intervention to fix those problems.

As discussed elsewhere in this chapter and in Chapter 16, check fraud is a huge problem. Incorporating the required procedures into the mix to prevent check fraud adds more costs to the equation.

Even the issue of mailing checks becomes complicated. They must be taken to the mailroom right before the mail is delivered to the post office. If taken earlier, the company is opening itself up to the possibility that the checks will be stolen. And if the checks don't go to the mailroom until the end of the day, where and how they are kept before that becomes an issue—again introducing more elaborate procedures (and therefore additional costs) into the check production process.

Getting checks signed is another hassle. A discussion of who can sign what checks and the dollar limits related to signing authority is for another book. Just know that getting checks signed using anything other than a signature plate as part of the check production process adds work and expense.

IDEAL (BEST PRACTICE) CHECK ISSUANCE SCENARIO

If all invoices are sent to one repository rather than various places throughout the organization, not only will the invoice handling process operate more smoothly, check problems will be reduced. Once accounts payable knows an invoice is "in process," it can better track the item. Better tracking reduces the likelihood of a duplicate invoice getting into the process.

Once the invoice has been approved and returned to accounts payable, whether it is on paper or electronic, the three-way match of the invoice against the receiving document and purchase order should be undertaken. Once any disputes, should they exist, have been resolved, the invoice should be scheduled for payment according to the agreed-on terms. This means that the due date indicated on the invoice may not agree with the date the invoice is scheduled for payment.

At the point that checks are to be run, the appropriate check stock should be retrieved. Check storage, printing, and signature practices are discussed later in this chapter. Once the checks are printed, they should be mailed as quickly as possible.

At the time checks are printed, a check issuance file for positive pay should be produced and transmitted to the issuing bank. Positive pay is discussed in Chapter 16 on check fraud.

Some checks may need a hand signature added to them. These should be separated from the rest and processed separately. The checks that do not require a hand signature should be mailed as soon as possible, reducing the opportunity for someone to filtch them.

In most cases the person printing the checks will take the checks to be mailed to the mailroom to be posted. Great care needs to be taken with this step. As mentioned, checks should not be delivered to the mailroom until right before they are taken to the post office. The reason for this is simple. In many organizations the mailroom is not secure. Many people wander in and out, and messengers and delivery people often come into the mailroom unrestricted. It doesn't take a rocket scientist to identify envelopes that contain checks. Leaving the checks around is an invitation to people with larceny in their hearts.

Checks that need a hand signature added need special handling. For starters, the backup needs to be reattached to the check so that the person signing can verify the check's veracity. No one should sign an item without documentation. With the documentation reattached, the checks should be presented to the authorized check signer for signature. Care needs to be taken here as some organizations have poor internal controls at this step. A few controls that should be integrated into your process are:

- Checks should never leave the premises.
- Checks should be kept under lock and key when not being signed.
- Signers should review backup before signing.
- Once signed, checks should be returned to accounts payable for processing and mailing.

The issue of the checks never leaving the premises needs to be reinforced with some check signers. Occasionally an overworked executive will decide to take checks home and sign them in the evening. If this seems like a reasonable practice, consider the consequences when this executive has her briefcase stolen or loses the checks. (And, yes, this has happened.)

Once signed, the backup needs to be removed and the checks mailed as described.

Checks should never be returned to the person who requested them. This issue is discussed in more detail later in this chapter.

CHECK STORAGE

How secure your check stock needs to be will depend in large part on the type of checks you use. If you use preprinted check stock, you must take great care. (This is discussed a little later in this chapter.) If, like a growing number of companies, you don't have the company and banking information printed on the check at the time the checks are printed, care of the check stock is less important. In fact, in theory, a check could be printed on any paper, although this is generally not recommended.

Preprinted check stock should be kept under lock and key with as few people as possible having access. The number should be limited to two or three so that there will always be someone available to open the closet should stock be needed. Additionally, a log should accompany the check stock. The log should be used to keep count of the check stock. Check numbers should be verified against the number of checks printed. The log should be initialed by parties witnessing the check printing process. Ideally, internal audit will do one or two surprise audits of the check stock against the log to ensure that no blank checks are missing. Every single check should be accounted for, whether used, waiting to be used, or voided. At a minimum:

- Access to the check stock should be severely limited.
- Checks should be stored in a secure, locked closet.
- The closet should be reinforced—and not of the type that a thief could easily hack into.
- The lock on the door should be substantial and not easily picked with a hairpin or clothes hanger.

Ideally, the check storage closet should not be in close proximity to the printer. If someone breaks in, especially on a long weekend, don't make it too easy for the thief.

Sufficient segregation of duties should be incorporated into the various tasks associated with the check production cycle, so that individuals with access to the check storage closet do not also have the authority to print checks. Clearly, anyone with access to the check storage closet should not be responsible for the reconciliation of the company's bank accounts.

CHECK STOCK

Whether you use blank check stock and print the banking information and company logo as part of the check printing process or use preprinted check stock, your checks should incorporate some security features to make it more difficult for thieves to copy them. A partial list of security features that can be incorporated into check stock follows.

- Microprinting
- Watermarks

- Ultra sensitive watermarks
- Holograms
- Foil strips
- Microprint lines
- Void pantograph
- Laid lines
- Warning banners to alert tellers to watermarks

There are other possible security features, but this gives you an idea of what is on the market today. Most experts feel that if you have incorporated at least three security features in your checks, you have exercised reasonable care.

You should also be aware that there have been several reports that the Void pantograph does not appear when copies are made on some of the newer copying machines.

Some experts recommend against including statements on checks such as "not valid for checks over a certain dollar limit." Including this statement helps only one person: the crook. A thief seeing a notice about a $500 limit will simply write the check for $499. This is not to say that such limits should not be set on accounts—just don't make the crook's job easier by putting the notice on the checks.

Some companies use numbered safety paper—a recommended best practice. This numbered paper incorporates many safety features. Each sheet of paper is sequentially numbered. A log is kept of the sequentially numbered safety paper.

WHY RETURNING CHECKS CAN BE A PROBLEM

Often in the corporate world, someone will request that rather than being mailed to the recipient, checks be returned to the requestor. This is a bad practice and a control point. Checks should not be returned to requestors for two simple reasons: It's inefficient, and it opens the door to fraud. If you are scratching your head about the fraud, consider this experience, which one of my newsletter readers wrote about.

> A former employee, who was in charge of all the trade show planning, would request checks to be processed, payable to the trade shows. The request was approved by the same person using the initials of their superior. This was common practice at that time, due to the lengthy traveling the superior does. Now when I think about it, how stupid were we to put that much trust in someone. We have a list of people allowed to sign the checks here, none are stamped. Those individuals signed these checks, trusting the former employee, and allowed me to return the checks to her believing they were getting sent to the trade shows.
>
> Never in my wildest dreams did I ever imagine it was possible for a check made payable to another business to be allowed to be deposited into a personal bank account. Five years into the situation, one of the VPs decided to find out why the trade shows were costing so much. We found out why. This ordeal cost the company a lot of money. Since then we have drastically changed our policies. *I will not give any check back to the requester*. The only exception to this rule is that specific requests must be signed off by an officer of the company.

This story emphasizes, once again, the old adage about fraud being committed by long-term, trusted employees. If you are still getting nowhere on this issue, you can always point out that under Sarbanes-Oxley, returning checks to requisitioners could be considered poor internal controls.

There are also practical considerations. Many times the check never gets mailed out to the vendor. Then accounts payable gets a call wondering where payment is. Occasionally the departments pick up the check and forget to mail out the check. Other times, checks get lost on the desk of the employee who picked them up.

By the way, if an alternative payment vehicle was used, this issue would never get raised.

A WORD ABOUT BANK STATEMENT RECONCILIATION

Bank statements should be reconciled within 30 days of their receipt if you want to be considered exercising reasonable care should a fraudulent check be discovered. Don't let this task get months behind, as sometimes happens in a busy corporate world where staff often is overworked. It's easy to let something like bank reconciliations get behind, but it is a bad practice.

Late bank reconciliations can be considered poor internal controls and could get you dinged in your Sarbanes-Oxley audit.

Finally, you cannot let just anyone do the bank reconciliations. Some companies have it handled in a department that does not produce checks, having checks handled in accounts payable and the reconciliation in treasury. Even if it is done in the same department, as frequently happens, the person doing the bank reconciliations should not have access to the check stock. Additionally, that person should not be involved in unclaimed property reporting, because that opens up the opportunity for fraud. Knowing what checks are outstanding on the bank reconciliations, a shady individual could report them as unclaimed property; then, when producing the report, change the name of the party who is owed the check to his or her own or that of an accomplice. This happened recently at one organization. It was uncovered because the employee, who was not overly bright, used his own name on a check in excess of $300,000. Thus, it stood out like a sore thumb. Had he been a little smarter about his theft, it might have gone undetected.

REALLY BAD CHECK PRACTICES

So many bad check practices abound in the corporate world, it would make your head spin. A few that you should avoid at all costs follow.

- Not appropriately storing check stock. Keeping blank check stock in a desk drawer or a file cabinet used by the entire staff is just begging for check fraud.
- Returning checks to anyone other than the payee.
- Making every employee over a certain level an authorized check signer.

- Not using positive pay.
- Making undocumented changes to source documents. One accounts payable professional related this story: "We have had cases where a check was cut and mailed, and then the requestor wanted to change the amount. The supervisor pulled the original check request, changed the amount based on the verbal request and processed the check again. The original check was not in AP's possession, and the change was never sent through the approval process. The original check was not voided nor stop paid so that positive payment processing would report it to the bank, causing it to come back as an exception if presented for payment. The supervisor should have requested a whole new check request and approval, and should have immediately stopped payment on the first check." We agree.
- Not accounting for blank or prenumbered checks comparing actual usage to what is in your computer.
- Signing blank checks. "I worked at a church and thank goodness I was honest!" another accounts payable manager stated. "The checks required two signatures. Rather than have me make out the checks and then have them looked over, one of the board members would sign six or eight checks every Sunday ahead of time. Any one of the other signers could have cleaned out the account. Of course I knew there wasn't much in there so I would not have been able to get very far over the border."

PAYMENT TRENDS

After years of complaints, organizations are starting to look for ways to reduce the number of paper checks they issue. However, it is likely that paper checks, albeit in reduced numbers, will be with us for a long time.

5

Traditional Electronic Methodology: Wire Transfers and Financial EDI

INTRODUCTION

Moving money electronically used to be a luxury in the business world, typically reserved for large-dollar transactions or last-minute rush payments when funds absolutely had to arrive the same day or perhaps the next. In some cases organizations married the electronic exchange of information related to purchase orders and invoices with the payment world, resulting in an electronic payment. This process is referred to as FEDI (financial electronic data interchange). Automated clearinghouse (ACH) payments are making an impact on the need for FEDI and wire transfers. In fact, banks are starting to look for ways to reduce their wire costs to attract back some of the business lost to ACH. It is doubtful that they will be successful.

WIRE TRANSFERS

The transaction cost of wire transfers relative to other payment alternatives can be as high as $50, although typically it is somewhat lower. In an era where alternative payment methodologies can be had for a tiny fraction of the cost, wire transfers are losing a lot of their appeal. When wire transfers are used, there tends to be more than one hand in the pot. Special consideration should be given to these issues:

- *Responsibility.* The first issue regarding wire transfers relates to where the responsibility for the function lies. This can be a serious consideration. In 50 to 75% of all organizations, the treasury group does the wire transfers, while checks are issued in accounts payable. In fact, in a recent Future of Accounts Payable survey completed by *Accounts Payable Now & Tomorrow*, only 29.67% of all accounts payable departments had sole responsibility for wire transfers in their organization. Another 30.77% shared the responsibility with other departments, while 34.07% had wires handled completely in another department. The remainder either didn't do wire transfers in their organization or did them so infrequently that they were not sure where they were handled.
- *A departmental coordination of efforts.* In those numerous instances where wire transfers are handled by a group different from those who are responsible for checks, there needs to be coordination between the two groups. Why? Because in more instances than anyone would like to admit in public, many invoices that are paid with a wire are then paid again with a check. One of the ways this happens is that when a payment is late, the vendor will insist on a wire transfer. Then, when the original invoice finally does show up, it gets paid. One way to avoid this is when the vendor screams for a wire transfer, try to convince them to take an ACH payment,

if that initiative is run by accounts payable. This will keep the cost down and perhaps reduce the risk of a duplicate payment.

- *Best practice recommendation.* Tighten controls and consider moving the responsibility for wire transfers to accounts payable, where other payments are originated. Those organizations in which wire transfers are initiated in more than one department are especially troubling. That is not a good idea and opens the door wide for trouble.
- *Types of wire transfers.* Wire transfers can be broken into two broad groups: those made on a recurring basis and one-time or irregularly made payments. This distinction is important when it comes to setting up wires online. It is also important when consideration is given to controls, fraud, and duplicate payment prevention.
- *Initiating a wire transfer.* Wire instructions can be sent to the bank online or by phone. Regardless of which initiation technique is used, the instructions need to be verified by a party other than the one who initiated the transaction. This is an important internal control point that is especially critical when it comes to preventing fraud. The list of people authorized to initiate wire transfers, as well as those authorized to approve the wires after they have been initiated, should be limited to a small group of individuals. As with signing checks, this is not something that all executives should automatically have authority to do.
- *Online wire transfers.* When wires are done online, the process typically involves typing in the requisite information. Each approved person should have his or her own user ID and password. While it is not rocket scientist work, it is a task that involves some responsibility. Rarely is this task assigned to a clerical person, but that does not mean that in some organizations clerical staff do not enter the data. Yes, that's

right—in some organizations the person who enters the data is not the one who is authorized to enter it. Unfortunately, this can lead to fraud.

Sharing passwords and user IDs is a very bad idea. Now, before you start to explain that the person in your organization who's been entering the wires, even though not authorized, is a long-term, trusted employee, consider this. Most employee fraud is committed by long-term, trusted employees.

- *Providing crooks with information—unintentionally, of course.* It is not uncommon for a company to receive a call asking for wire instructions by someone looking to pay the company. Most of the time these are legitimate requests. However, occasionally, they are not. Thieves have figured out that calling and asking for wire instructions by claiming they are getting ready to pay a company is one of the easiest ways to get a company's bank account number. And they are correct. Most organizations will provide the information without giving the call a second thought.
- *Limitations on wire transfer accounts.* Therefore, some companies use one account for wires and another for checks. If someone tries to write a check against the wire transfer account, it will bounce because the wire account cannot honor checks. Although this is not a Sarbanes-Oxley requirement per se, it is a good internal control point and could help you avoid getting dinged in the audit. In fact, all organizations should use this approach.
- *Wires initiated by phone.* Periodically it will be necessary to call a wire transfer in to the bank. This should be only done in emergency cases, as it is a weak process from a control standpoint. Before the wire is released, the bank will call back a second individual at the company to verify the information. The person authorized to verify has been preestablished by the company and his or her name has been provided to

the bank in advance. Basically, this process relies on voice recognition, which is not great. This control gets even weaker when the party who is the primary contact is out and the backup verifier provides the authorization.

- *Repetitive wire transfers.* These transfers are made routinely to the same parties. Often they are trusted or key vendors as well as related parties. The banking information can be set up ahead of time so instead of relaying all that information each time the transfer is made, it is only necessary to provide an access number or reference number. Typically, only the dollar amount changes on these transfers. The philosophy behind these transfers is that even if the money goes to the wrong party, getting it back will not be an issue. Almost always, these transactions are handled over the Internet using a personal computer. After the first party enters the information, a second person "releases" the transfers by entering his or her own unique password and user ID.
- *Nonrepetitive wire transfers.* Conversely, nonrepetitive transfers are made on a one-shot basis to parties that the organization does not have an ongoing regular payment relationship with. They must be verified by a second party before the payments are released. These transactions can be initiated either by phone or over the Internet using a personal computer.
- *Sharing passwords.* Sharing passwords is a really bad idea from an internal control standpoint. It makes it impossible to verify who initiated or released the payment. In some organizations it is a firing offense. Each person who works with the organization's wire transfers should have his or her own unique password and user ID. These employees' integrity should never be put at risk by asking them to share.
- *Funds availability.* For domestic wire transfers initiated before 3 P.M., good funds will be available the same day. Sometimes this is referred to as same-day availability. On the international front, it will take longer. Contrast this with

ACH transfers, which usually result in funds being available on the following day. The price differential between wire transfers and ACH is so great that it is worth the small effort involved in planning to use ACH to get your funds where they should be within the requisite time frame.

- *Common use.* Wires are still in use for real estate transactions where title cannot pass until the funds are in the selling party's bank account. Typically, a confirmation code, sometimes referred to as a reference number, is provided as proof the funds were sent.
- *Separate wire bank accounts.* As mentioned, a separate bank account should be set up for incoming wire transfers. That way, when crooks get the information, they cannot use it to initiate a phony check. While many organizations initiate wire transfers out of a different bank account from the one on which they write checks, the imperative is not quite as strong, as organizations rarely provide this information to outsiders who call. Still, many have a separate account for this activity.

FINANCIAL EDI

EDI, or electronic data interchange, is the term used to describe the electronic transfer of information in a standardized, computer-readable format. Organizations and their trading partners sometimes use EDI to exchange purchase orders, invoices, and other business documents. To transfer this information electronically, the trading partners typically will use a value-added network (VAN), a third-party communications network that allows trading partners to send and receive their business transaction information electronically. Sometimes you will hear reference to a VAB (value-added bank), which is a bank acting in this capacity.

Both EDI and financial EDI (FEDI) can be used to replace traditional paper documents, but FEDI can also include the electronic transfer of funds. When FEDI includes a payment, a financial institution must be used to facilitate the transfer of funds, which is usually accomplished via the ACH network. (The National Automated Clearing House Association [NACHA] rules govern which ACH payment formats may be used to send EDI through the ACH.)

In its time, FEDI was definitely an innovation that helped some organizations become more efficient. However, most that used it relied heavily on expensive mainframe computers, and their systems often needed expensive modifications to handle the data. Frankly, that was a good part of the impetus for the genesis of VANs. Expense was definitely a factor that kept EDI from growing as fast or as large as some of its early proponents would have liked. The other complaint revolved around the inflexibility of the process. The rigidity related to data transfer space limitations, and thus the limited explanations that could be provided.

Trading partners participating in FEDI are able to send the information and payment separately or together. If the payment and information are sent separately, the information typically will be sent through a VAN, while the payment will be sent by a financial institution through the ACH. If the information accompanies the payment, the payment-related information, such as a remittance advice, will be placed in an addenda record attached to the ACH item. Either the sending corporation or its financial institution will put this addenda information in standardized, computer-readable format.

As with any other new process, a new "language" developed. ACH payment "formats" for the business-to-business (B2B) world include the CCD-Plus and CTX formats used for corporate payments. The CCD stands for Cash Concentration Disbursement and the plus refers to plus addendum while CTX stands for Corporate Trade Exchange. A number of standardized formatted messages, commonly referred to as X12 transaction sets, have been developed for different applications. These transaction sets are the electronic equivalent of paper documents. The NACHA rules govern which transaction sets may be sent through the ACH.

In the payment world, the two most common transaction sets are the 810, which represents an invoice or billing information, and the 820, which has remittance advice information on it.

Doing Business with the Federal Government?

You may have to use EDI, whether you like it or not, because Congress mandated that most payments by the federal government would be electronic by January 1, 1999.

Impact of the Internet on EDI

Most of what has been written in this chapter about EDI was put in place before the Internet because such a powerful force in the business arena. Clearly, if the Internet had come into play a decade or two earlier, EDI might not ever have found its place in the corporate arena. But it is here. A number of large corporations (the 800-pound gorillas in their markets) have made large financial investments in their EDI systems, and they are not going to flush these away just because something cheaper and more flexible shows up. Some of its proponents found ways to marry the Internet technology with EDI to deliver a more efficient product—and perhaps keep alive the product in which they had a vested interest. Since Internet-based technology is much cheaper than the traditional models, it is not surprising that businesses and people would flock to it. This approach is referred to as EDI over the Internet or Web EDI.

Payment Trend

Both wire transfers and EDI have a shrinking place in the current payment arena. Wires will continue to have a place in those instances where it is imperative that funds be transferred on the same day. We do not expect this requirement to go away completely. But, because of the cost of wire transfers, their use will be limited. Although EDI will hold onto a place in the current marketplace, it is unlikely to grow unless it can find a way to reinvent itself into a cost-efficient model that can compete with the Internet.

6

P-CARDS

INTRODUCTION

Although p-cards started out as a vehicle for organizations looking for a way to handle small-dollar invoices, they are quickly finding a place in the payment arena, and often their place is anything but minor. As organizations become comfortable with the cards and get over their fears of excessive inappropriate use by their employees, they are quickly growing to love the reduction in the number of invoices processed in accounts payable combined with the attractive rebate feature.

BACKGROUND

P-cards, also referred to as procurement cards or corporate procurement cards, are similar to charge cards and operate very much like the credit card you have in your wallet. They are given to those employees who regularly make purchases on behalf of your organization. They should not be given automatically to all employees over a certain level, only those whose jobs require that they regularly make purchases on behalf of the company.

REBATES

Once a program has been set up correctly and volume builds, organizations can earn rebates based on their volume. This is not information that card issuers will volunteer. In fact, just a few years ago, companies receiving these rebates were required to sign a non disclosure agreement in which they agreed not to divulge that they were getting a rebate or the amount. That is no longer required. Rebates are often a negotiating point so don't necessarily take the first amount offered. When shopping for a new card issuer, ask about rebate policy.

Although a certain volume is generally required in order to qualify for a rebate, the minimum level to meet the requirement has dropped precipitously. Today monthly charge volume of $50,000 qualifies; in some cases even less. Accounts payable departments that generally get these rebates sometimes share them with other departments to encourage card usage. In other cases, accounts payable is retaining the rebates, using them to fund other enhancement programs or to buy technology for which there is no budget allocation.

HOW THE P-CARD PROCESS SHOULD WORK

There's no one set way that every best practice card program will operate. Corporate culture and unique organizational or industry requirements will impact the programs. However, some guidelines are appropriate. The National Association of Purchasing Card Professionals (NAPCP) recommends that:

- Plastic purchasing cards or nonplastic account numbers are issued to requisitioners.
- Each card/account is mapped to a general ledger (G/L) account. (In some cases G/L mapping can be done based on merchant category codes or point-of-sale information.)
- The requisitioner places orders with suppliers providing appropriate payment instructions.

- The supplier processes the order using its acquiring bank's authorization process.
- Cardholders receive their purchasing card statement directly from the card issuer. The cardholder reviews and approves the statement. Cardholders do not submit a payment.
- A single electronic invoice is sent from the card issuer to the requisitioner's organization on a monthly, weekly, or daily basis. The invoice is processed to create accounting entries and facilitate payment.

INDIVIDUAL LIMITS

One of the control features in the cards is the ability to set individual limits. Again, these should relate to job functionality and requirements, not title. Some of the ways companies control p-card usage while simultaneously encouraging employees to use it wherever possible are:

- *Limit the dollar amount of each transaction.* Some companies set this limit as low as $50 or $100 to start. When they become more comfortable with the program or want to grow it, they increase the limits. There are those who have limits as high as $5,000, and a few have no limits.
- *Limit the dollar amount that each employee can spend in a given month.* A repairperson might be limited to no more than $1,000 per month while the plant supervisor might have a limit that is 10 times that amount. Limits can be set low initially and then raised as needed. Remember, this level is not related to an individual's title.
- *Use Standard Industrial Code (SIC) blocks.* For example, some companies block furriers and other luxury goods stores. The problem with this issue is that sometimes companies are in more than one line of business, yet they are limited to one SIC code. There have been instances where employees have

been blocked from making legitimate purchases. Only use SIC blocks if you are concerned about inappropriate use.

- *Insist that the manager review and sign off on all monthly statements.* Remind managers that their signature makes them equally responsible for inappropriate charges.

Additionally, there should be a periodic review by someone independent of the cardholder.

1099 REPORTING

This is an ugly issue but it must be raised. Paying for a service with a credit card does not negate an organization's obligation to report income paid to independent contractors. What's more, if some of those payments are made by check and others on a p-card, the two amounts must be aggregated and reported on one Form 1099.

There is some talk that the card issuers will take over this responsibility under Qualified Purchase Card Agents (QPCA). As of this writing in spring 2007, that has not happened. Those making the payments are still required to report the income.

This issue has an even uglier side than might appear at first glance. Often institutions that one might think are corporations are not. In particular, hotels that are part of major chains often are owned individually. Technically, this payment should be reported. So, while the credit card receipt might say Marriott or Sheraton, in actuality the payment might be going to a franchisee who owns that particular branch. Of course, this issue would arise regardless of the payment methodology used. To date, no perfect solution to this thorny issue has been developed.

PALMER P-CARD 2005 SURVEY: HIGHLIGHTS

Speaking at NAPCP's seventh annual conference, Dr. Richard Palmer revealed the results of the 2005 Palmer and Gupta 2003 Purchasing Card Benchmark Survey. He was the first to point out that the survey results are somewhat slanted since those filling out the survey are, for the most part, high-end p-card users. However, a snapshot of some of the highlights of that survey provides insights into how p-cards are being used today and what can be expected in the future.

- The p-card approach is moving to smaller organizations as the concept becomes more widely accepted.
- Most organizations using p-cards are increasing the spend on their cards.
- Per annum growth over the next few years should average in the 10 to 15% range.
- The survey identified several emerging goals including:
  - An increased control for the card
  - The ability to get data from the card
  - Rebates
  - Getting more suppliers to accept p-cards as well as expanding the boundaries of those who already accept them.
- There are fewer cards in most programs, but cards in existence generally have a higher spend on them.
- When looking at the payback from the cards, Dr. Palmer asked respondents if their card program were dropped, how many more people would their organizations have to hire. Respondents indicated that there would be an increase of 63% on the accounts payable staff and 61% on the purchasing side. Palmer calls p-cards "the gift that keeps on giving."
- Of the respondents, 25% reported that they had used the card data for discount negotiations.
- Respondents were also able to reduce the number of vendors in the master vendor file as well as the activity in petty cash boxes.
- A lot of potential growth opportunities exist in programs. Palmer estimated that if everything under $2,500 were put on the card, the programs would triple in size.

- Some of the numerical trends presented by Dr. Palmer are:
  - Average spend/month: $1.3 million
  - Median monthly spend/card: $260,000
  - Average monthly spend/card: $1831
  - Average transaction size: $263
  - Average number of transactions/month/card: 7

As you can see from the numbers presented, there is still a lot of potential for p-cards in the business environment. Consider that:

- Cardholders are looking to expand the boundaries of where the card is used.
- Average transaction size is relatively small.
- Cost savings associated with the programs (versus checks) are impressive.
- Companies continue to look for ways to cut costs.

It is only reasonable to assume that programs will continue to expand as organizations look to, yet again, do more with less.

COMMON P-CARD PITFALLS

Like other corporate initiatives, not every p-card program launched is a success. Some fail simply because the people implementing the program neglected to anticipate everything that possibly could go wrong. Sometimes the problem could have been avoided if only the issue had been addressed before the program was launched. So, you may be wondering, just what are the issues that are most likely to doom a p-card program if not addressed before its inception?

Speaking at the Information Reporting and Accounts Payable conference run by IRSCompliance.org and *Accounts Payable Now & Tomorrow*, the NAPCP's Lynn Larson took aim at that very topic. Her information is based both on personal experience and the many conversations she's had with members of the National

Association of Purchasing Card Professionals, most of whom are practitioners.

Based on this insight, Larson identified the most common reasons p-card programs falter:

- *Administrator not suited for position.* Rarely is thought given to the skills needed to administer a p-card program. The person chosen is occasionally not suited for the position.
- *Lack of infrastructure and management support.* Like any other corporate initiative, if management support is lacking, the program will have a diminished chance for success. Hand in hand with management support goes the infrastructure necessary to run a program. If management's attitude is that this is something that the accounts payable manager can run off the side of their desk, the program is likely to run into trouble or remain dismally small.
- *Ineffective training.* Training is crucial. If it is overlooked, end users will make mistakes, which will lead them to avoid the p-card as a payment alternative. Additionally, they may not take full advantage of all the opportunities the cards offer. This will result in less than optimal usage.
- *Unclear policies and procedures.* If it is not made crystal clear how the card is to be used and what is expected from end users, there will be trouble. It is inevitable that one or more of your end users will find a way to unintentionally misuse the card. When the matter erupts, as it inevitably will, that end user will dig in his or her heels and try to find ways *not* to use the card in the future. And then, of course, there are the employees who will intentionally use the card inappropriately because "no one told them they couldn't do that."
- *Lack of communication to suppliers.* It is crucial that suppliers that are to be paid with the card know that and adjust their invoicing processes accordingly. Otherwise, they will generate invoices that may unintentionally get paid in your shop, resulting in a duplicate payment.

- *Over-or undercontrolling the program.* Finding the right level of controls for your p-card program is not easy but is critical to its success. If not enough controls are instituted in the program, employees could end up p-cards in ways you really don't want them to. However, if you micromanage the program, potential end users may get disgusted and look for ways to sabotage it.
- *Too many manual processes.* One of the goals of a p-card program is to simplify the payment process. This should not be done at someone else's expense. It should not make things more complicated for the end user. If it does, they'll find ways not to use their cards. Manual processes will tend to do this. Too many manual processes could doom your program.
- *Too many inactive accounts.* At first glance, inactive accounts may not seem like a problem, but they are. A large number of inactive accounts signals that end users are not using their cards or that you are giving cards to employees who don't need them. Neither of these is a good thing. Monitor the cards that are inactive and educate the end user regarding proper use, if appropriate.

Even the most conscientious program administrator will occasionally run into problems. It is probably not realistic to expect to avoid all problems. Larson offers seven suggestions to help when your program doesn't run as smoothly as you'd like—despite all your meticulous planning:

1. Address any resistance to existing program.
2. Do not make p-cards difficult to use or administer.
3. Correct any infrastructure issues.
4. Ensure that current controls are effective.
5. Refine and implement procedures where lacking.
6. Resolve existing technology problems and automate as many processes as possible.
7. Address where program management resources are lacking.

P-CARD DATA

Once you start building volume in your p-card program, you will become aware of the importance of getting detailed data from the card issuer. This helps update the G/L. It is also useful for your purchasing staff when it comes time to negotiate contracts with suppliers. Information comes in three levels:

Level 1: Basic Credit Card Information. Level 1 data is similar to the information you would find on your personal credit card statement. This information includes:

Date
Supplier
Dollar amount

Level 2: Customer-Defined Transaction Data. Transactions that include Level 2 data include Level 1 data plus:

Sales tax
Variable data field

Suppliers that are Level 2 capable have the ability to pass sales tax information as well as a unique transaction data field (typically limited to 16 characters) through the purchasing card system. Some issuers pass this data to the cardholder statement. Level 2 data can be extremely helpful to the cardholder in reconciling charges, especially in the case of repetitive charges. Examples of Level 2 variable data include:

- An order number
- An employee name (in the case of temporary service provider)
- A sample number (in the case of providers of laboratory testing service)

Level 3: Line Item Detail. Transactions that include Level 3 data include Levels 1 and 2 data plus:

Item product code
Item description
Item quantity

Item unit of measure
Item price
Item tax

The more information you can get from a card issuer, the better. However, if your system is not set up to accept that information, it is pointless to focus on it. Also, keep in mind that the card issuer may have the capability of providing you that data, but if the supplier does not collect it, there is nothing the card issuer can do. If this information is important to you, the purchasing team can make it a requirement when negotiating new contracts.

FRAUD PREVENTION

When p-cards first appeared on the scene, some executives refused to have the program in their shop because they were concerned that their employees would use the cards for personal purchases. Others didn't go that far but were extremely restrictive in who was given cards for basically the same reason. These fears were exaggerated. Yes, p-card fraud does occasionally occur, but then, so do other types of employee fraud.

Managers are urged to set up programs that have fraud protections built in. Some guidelines that will help include:

- *Create a detailed cardholder agreement requiring the signature of the cardholder and the cardholder's supervisor.* The agreement should contain a statement that the employee acknowledges the company's right to fire him or her if the employee uses the card inappropriately. Although the primary responsibility for using the card appropriately lies with the cardholder, the supervisor has the ultimate accountability for how the card is used. Should someone flagrantly misuse the card, his or her employment should be terminated, and this fact should be made public. Unfortunately, sometimes it is necessary to set an example to show that you are serious about enforcing the policy.

- *Create a detailed policies and procedures manual and update it regularly to reflect the p-card program roles and responsibilities accurately.* This document can be put online so everyone who may need to access it can do so. The manual not only spells out everyone's responsibilities; it also provides the framework for the entire administrative process, including internal controls and fraud prevention.
- *Appoint a permanent administrator responsible for the p-card program.* The administrator will ensure that all aspects of the card program are kept up to date and reflect the most current technology and management controls available. This person will also be responsible for training and retraining cardholders and transaction reconcilers, as well as monitoring for incidences of possible unintentional personal use or obvious misuse.
- *If possible, design the card so employees won't accidentally mistake it for one of their own personal cards.* If it looks like any other MasterCard, VISA, or American Express card, it is an easy mistake to make. If your program is large enough, you may be able to get your logo put on the card. Recognize that honest mistakes do happen, but they occur very rarely.
- *Establish reasonable card limits to reduce excessive or inappropriate use issues.* Again, just because someone is a vice president, if the job does not require a $10,000 line, don't give it to the person. There's no sense tempting fate. While 99 times out of 100 there will be no problem, why open the door to temptation?
- *Require training before issuing a p-card to a new cardholder, and require refresher training at least every two years for continuing cardholders.* The training can be face-to-face or computer/Web-based. Some organizations insist that it be face-to-face for new cardholders, but that is not always logistically possible.

- *Require original receipts for all purchases made on the p-card.* Every receipt doesn't have to be checked, but spot check, and if you are at all suspicious, check all the receipts from the individual. Every photocopy increases the risk of fraud or abuse.
- *Provide an anonymous hotline process to report suspected abuse.* Every two years the Association of Certified Fraud Examiners (ACFE) produces a survey on occupational fraud called "Report to the Nation." In the 2006 report, the top ways fraud was uncovered were by an anonymous tip 34.2% of the time and by accident 25.4% of the time. Can you really afford *not* to have a tip line? Make sure you publicize this fact through your training.
- *Have meaningful and enforced policies governing consequences for misuse.* As discussed earlier, if intentional fraud is uncovered, the employee should be terminated. If it is possible, legal action should be pursued. This may seem harsh, but it is important that your employees know there are consequences. The fraudster should be prosecuted, and the prosecution should be publicized. Not prosecuting and publicizing thefts only increases the chances that culprits will do it again.
- *Establish a recurring audit process to evaluate compliance with program policies and requirements.* Although routine monitoring is best handled by each operating unit's management, regular surprise audits of card usage will deter fraud significantly.
- *Regularly review and update your policies and procedures as well as the limits on each card.* This review does not necessarily mean that limits will be increased. If they are not being reached, they can and should be decreased.
- *Don't overlook the ability to increase limits seasonally if your business requires such action.* The limits can be lowered once the high season has passed.

Payment Trends

P-cards will continue to play a significant role in the payment arena in the years to come. Organizations that learn how to fit them into the mix will do well—and may even find ways to add to the bottom line through an aggressive approach to rebates.

7

OTHER CREDIT CARDS ORGANIZATIONS USE TO PAY BILLS

INTRODUCTION

Certain business functions lend themselves to payment by credit cards. These functions mimic the times when purchase cards (p-cards) are used in general. The two that come most readily to mind are employees purchasing fuel and employee travel. In each case you have an individual making relatively small-dollar purchases in order to complete a company assignment. Here the definition of "small dollar" might go as high as several thousand dollars.

FUEL CARDS

An organization that has a fleet of cars or trucks will also need to make regular purchases of fuel. Depending on the nature of the business, this refueling may take place all over the country or it may take place on company premises. Either of these cases lends itself to the use of a fuel card (i.e., credit card that is used exclusively for fuel).

In certain instances, the card helps the company monitor usage. In others, it is simply a mechanism to keep fuel in the vehicles without having to worry about drivers being stranded without cash.

In any event, fuel cards are limited in that only a small percentage of organizations will use them. But when they are required, they help the organization fill a very real need.

T&E CARDS

A much more common card is the travel and entertainment (T&E) card. This is used to help employees pay for T&E expenses when conducting company business. There is no one single way that all organizations pay for travel. Here's a rundown of the various ways in which organizations pay for employee travel:

- Employees use their own credit card and are completely responsible for obtaining the credit card and paying the bill.
- A company T&E card is used with the employee responsible for paying the bill.
- A company T&E card is used with the employee responsible for paying the bill but the company guaranteeing the payment and making payment should the employee default.
- A company T&E card is used with the company paying the bill.

Reality

In most instances, employees must use their own cards. In a recent *Accounts Payable Now & Tomorrow* survey, over half (53.52%) of the companies responding indicated that they don't give employees a T&E card. Even if the company does provide the card, the employee isn't off the hook. At slightly over half (58%) of the companies issuing cards, the company makes the payment.

At the 42% of the companies that offer cards payment, responsibility is:

Employee	29%
Employee, but company must pay if employee defaults	13%
Company	58%

Payments

Many employees like to use their own credit cards because they rack up frequent-flyer miles or other goodies based on the dollar amounts put on the cards. Some question whether it is fair to expect employees to use their own credit for the benefit of the company. Also, employees with limited credit availability might end up strapped for personal expenditures if they have used their credit for the company.

There is another issue with the use of a personal credit card. It provides deceitful employees with a mechanism to defraud their companies. Because they can charge and receive refunds for many things on the card, the employer has to check certain things extra thoroughly.

Policy Compliance

One of the really nice features of some of the new T&E programs that are emerging is their ability to monitor T&E reimbursement requests for policy compliance. The best will flag requests that are outside the policy. A few will not permit a request that is outside the formal company policy. This feature is good for the company, as it helps keep costs under control and is a boon for the department, usually accounts payable, responsible for handling the reimbursement requests.

Ideally, if T&E expenditures are rolled into the p-card program for a one-card approach, this feature will not be lost in the process. T&E policy compliance—or rather lack of policy compliance—is a problem for some organizations. It would be a shame to see those that had started using this electronic monitoring give it up just to get an increased rebate. Ideally, they would pay with the one card but continue to use the T&E process that included the online policy compliance monitoring.

WHY FUEL AND T&E CARDS MAKE SENSE

The beauty of fuel and T&E cards is that they help the organization track and monitor spending. This can be critical when it comes to negotiating contracts with preferred vendors. The ability to aggregate the numbers and provide them to prospective suppliers should not be underestimated.

The cards also allow an organization to tailor programs to meet its unique travel and fuel needs. This could become more difficult if the cards are melded into a one-card approach, as is discussed next.

Both fuel and T&E cards can be put under the supervision of the professional who best understands those issues. This might not be the case should these expenditures be bundled into a "one" card.

ONE CARDS

Having discussed some of the reasons why individual T&E and fuel cards make sense, let's discuss the big reason that organizations like one cards. What used to be a much-whispered secret is now out in the open. Credit card companies offer rebates to their corporate clients that use their cards for significant volume. When this approach was started, companies needed a monthly volume of at least $500,000 to qualify. I have recently heard of card issuers that will give rebates to organizations charging $50,000 per month on average. The level will probably go lower.

This is one of the few ways that an accounts payable department can generate some revenue for their organization. Those who aggressively pursue that rebate continue to look for ways to increase the spend on the cards. It didn't take them long to turn their eyes toward their spending on T&E and fuel cards. For many companies, this was a no-brainer way to get a larger rebate.

Thus was born the one card. Organizations with fuel programs started putting their fuel purchases on this one card instead of their fuel cards.

Should you decide to go the one-card route and bundle in your T&E and fuel spending, make sure you review the strictures on your p-card program to ensure that your travelers and drivers don't run into some unexpected problems. Restrictions that might have made sense when you were running a traditional p-card program might not make sense in the T&E world. Take a close look at your daily limits and Merchant Category Code (MCC) blocking and daily limits.

When they first set up a p-card program, many organizations block numerous MCC codes. More than occasionally that includes hotels, resorts, and restaurants. Even resort blocking can cause travelers a problem, as many conferences are held at resorts. Thus, your traveler might be in for a rude awakening when he or she tries to check into the hotel.

Don't overlook bars, clubs, and sporting events. While you might not want your employees going to bars at the company's expense, your salespeople might regularly take potential clients out for an evening's entertainment.

Also consider your daily limits. Remember, hotel bills are typically paid at the end of the stay in one lump sum. It is not too hard to receive a hotel bill in excess of $1,000—especially if the stay is in a big city and is for several days. If the traveler also took clients to dinner at the hotel, the bill could be higher than your daily limit.

These are some of the more obvious issues. You might have some that are unique to your company or industry. Thus, if you should decide to go for the higher rebate by including T&E and fuel, carefully review the restrictions on your existing p-card account to ensure that your travelers will not run into trouble.

Of course, if you are setting up a new program, you will not have to worry about old restraints but will need to carefully plan out how you want the new program to be structured.

PUSHING THE P-CARD ENVELOPE: VARIANTS ON THE BASIC CARD

Organizations are using p-cards in a number of new ways. Without a doubt, p-cards have made the work of many accounts payable departments more manageable. When you combine the ease of use, the work reduction, and the rebate feature, it's no surprise that organizations everywhere have devised inventive variations on their use. A list of ways organizations are using p-cards follows.

- *Ghost cards.* An account designated for use by a certain department or supplier for a specific function/purpose.
- *Project cards.* The available balance declines as a card is used until dollars are depleted.
- *Accounts payable (AP) cards.* Cards given to the accounts payable staff to pay small-dollar invoices submitted for payment.

Payment Trends

Whether it makes overall sense or not, the rebate will continue to be a driving force for a good number of organizations. Thus, we expect to see volume on p-cards grow for the foreseeable future. That growth often will come as companies find ways to roll in T&E and fuel spending.

8

E-PAYMENTS (DIRECT PAYMENTS)

INTRODUCTION

People who get their paychecks directly deposited into their bank account are part of the electronic payment revolution. In fact, mimicking the direct deposit terminology that most people are familiar with, NACHA (the National Automated Clearing House Association) recently named payments made electronically through the ACH "direct payments." NACHA, the Electronic Payments Association, is responsible for electronic payments that go through its local networks.

AUTOMATED CLEARING HOUSE NETWORK

The Automated Clearing House (ACH) Network is a nationwide batch-oriented electronic funds transfer system governed by NACHA. It provides for the interbank clearing of electronic payments for participating depository financial institutions. The Federal Reserve and Electronic Payments Network act as ACH operators, central clearing facilities through which financial institutions transmit or receive ACH entries.

NACHA represents more than 11,000 financial institutions through direct memberships and a network of regional payments associations, and 650 organizations through its industry councils.

ACH payments include:

- Direct deposit of payroll, Social Security and other government benefits, and tax refunds
- Direct payment of consumer bills such as mortgages, loans, utility bills, and insurance premiums
- Business-to-business (B2B) payments
- E-checks
- E-commerce payments
- Federal, state, and local tax payments

Most of what is written about electronic payments in this book will fall under the heading of B2B payments.

For those readers who may want to peg their campaigns to grow their programs to some sort of a national initiative, May is Direct Deposit and Direct Payment month.

ACH PAYMENT GROWTH

Nearly 14 billion automated clearing house (ACH) payments were made in 2005, a 16.2% increase over 2004, according to statistics compiled by NACHA. Annual ACH payment volume has doubled in the last five years, spurred by growth across all transaction categories.

Interestingly, the biggest growth has come on the consumer side, as consumers embrace online bill payment options in record numbers and newer applications used primarily to collect their bill payments. Examples of this might be a bank debiting an individual's bank account for monthly mortgage or insurance payments.

Business Payments

Organizations of all sorts use the ACH Network for payments to and from trading partners, vendor payments, business-to-government tax withholdings, intracompany cash management transfers, and to exchange remittance information regarding payments.

The total number of B2B ACH payments grew to 2.0 billion in 2005, up 11.3% over 2004. Financial electronic data interchange—the electronic exchange of payment-related information or financial-related documents in standard formats between business partners on the ACH Network—grew by 19.8% in 2005. In that year there were 915 million electronic data interchange (EDI)–formatted remittance records accompanying ACH payments. The number of financial EDI payments in 2005 was 255.6 million, up 20.3% over 2004.

TYPES OF ACH PAYMENTS

As indicated, ACH payments can either be debits or credits. An organization can either initiate the payment itself or allow the payee to initiate the transaction. If it sends its bank the appropriate information to make the payment, an ACH credit has occurred. However, if you provide your banking information to your supplier and allow the supplier to initiate the payment by taking the funds from your account, an ACH debit transaction has occurred.

While the net result is the same, not everyone is comfortable in allowing vendors to debit their accounts. In fact, this debiting is most likely to occur if a taxing authority is involved or if there is a captive relationship between the vendor and the customer. Of course, there are also those instances where an 800-pound-gorilla vendor demands to be paid in this manner and the customer has no choice but to agree.

Most organizations that do allow debits from their accounts do so only on a very limited basis. They also generally set up a separate account just for this purpose.

ISSUES TO CONSIDER

As discussed in Chapter 2, checks are costly and create lots of problems. Electronic payments are definitely cheaper—10 cents an item by most estimates—and create far fewer problems. Here are a few considerations to take into account when deciding to make the move away from paper:

- *Float.* Since the payment you initiate today will hit the payee's bank tomorrow, the mail and processing float are squeezed out of the equation. Some who find this objectionable, despite all the other savings, have renegotiated payment terms with their suppliers to make the transactions float neutral. For the most part, the float period is split. Since most people believe that mail and processing float is about five days, adding two or three days to the payment terms is generally considered acceptable. However, this should be discussed with suppliers rather than taken arbitrarily.
- *Bank account reconciliations.* Since there should be no outstanding items, bank account reconciliations should be easier for these items.
- *Fraud issues.* While a move to electronic payments will certainly reduce check fraud problems, it will not completely eliminate all payment fraud concerns. It would be naive to think that all fraud considerations would disappear. ACH fraud currently is at a much lower level than check fraud, but it does exist. Steps you can and should take to guard against ACH fraud are discussed in Chapter 17. Note that some of these steps should be taken whether your organization makes electronic payments or not.

- *Strong up-front controls.* Since there is no signature on the payment, strong up-front controls are crucial as there is no signer "available" to catch errors. While it is true that signers shouldn't be catching mistakes, in reality they often do.
- *Escheat.* Since there are no uncashed checks, there are no escheat issues related to payments made this way.
- *Vendors.* There are vendor issues related to cash application. While one would think that vendors would be clamoring to be paid electronically, this has not turned out to be the case. Apparently some systems have trouble applying cash received electronically. Thus, some of your vendors may be reluctant to accept payments electronically despite the obvious benefits.
- *Staff reluctance to change.* As with any new initiative, expect to find some of your staff dragging their feet and complaining about the change. It goes with the territory.
- *Headcount.* The reality is once your program is up and running, you'll need fewer people to process payments, if you've managed to convert a significant portion of your vendors to the process. However, don't jump the gun. Getting vendors on board to the electronic payment program will take time and effort. Thus, initially you may need more people if you want to make one big push. This is one of the reasons many organizations slowly add vendors to their electronic payment program.

BEST PRACTICES TO AVOID ACH PAYMENT CONVERSION NIGHTMARES

If you do not execute your ACH payment conversion carefully, you could end up dooming the program before it has a chance to start. Learning from others' mishaps is one way to avoid making the same mistakes yourself. Unfortunately, often people are not willing to share their horror stories. One such story is about an organization that had a terrible time converting vendors to receive ACH payment. Some of the issues that could have been handled better include:

- *Master vendor file.* Not cleaning up the vendor database before requesting (actually demanding) that the vendors convert from check payments to ACH can lead to huge problems. The example organization had multiple active vendor codes in the system for the same vendors. It used SAP with one company code for multiple business areas.

  A huge disadvantage to the one-code-for-multiple-areas method is that when a payment proposal is done for one business area, the vendor will rarely realize it was only for one business area, not the entire company. If, for example, vendor code 123 is in the proposal for business area ABC, when business area DEF runs its proposal, vendor code 123 will be blocked to them. SAP does not give you an error message or any type of notice that it has blocked certain vendors—you just have to be on top of it to know if you're expecting a vendor to be paid and it doesn't come up in your proposal.

  That's a long-winded explanation, but it is the primary reason the example organization had so many active duplicate vendor codes. In addition, the method used for converting vendors to ACH was not very vendor friendly.

  For example, Vendor ABC sells raw materials to eight of the firm's divisions. It had eight different vendor codes set up in SAP due to the blocking issue just described. A list of all of vendors and their addresses was obtained from SAP by business area. So the company had eight different lists, each one showing ABC once. As each list was processed separately, ABC received eight different requests (and threats) to send their banking information or else! A cutoff date was named after which the company would no longer be issuing checks to them.

Here's the kicker. ABC Company would say, "Mm, sounds pretty good, sign me up!" and fill out one of the forms. After all, it only has one bank account. ABC would send along a copy of the company W-9, which was also requested (not because it was needed for the ACH conversion, but to update records). This was probably the only thing the firm did right. The vendor would send back one form and one W-9. Each form had the vendor's number on it. The company only updated the one vendor number that was on the one form ABC sent back—not all eight vendor numbers. Therefore, one vendor code was changed to ACH, the other seven received a threatening second request letter (which they ignored since they thought they had already responded) and continued to receive check payments until the company put them on payment block and quit paying them altogether. You can imagine how well this went over.

- *Getting accurate bank information.* Another big mistake was not requiring a copy of a canceled check to enter the ACH information from. The company accepted handwritten forms. This is a huge no-no. First, people get ACH payments and wire transfers confused. To the vendors, they are one and the same. To the banks, they are not. Many people gave the American Bankers Association (ABA) routing number for wire transfers and the ACH payment was rejected which wreaked havoc on the company's computer systems. The staff spent many frustrating hours on phone calls trying to explain the difference to people only to wind up calling their banks in the end anyway.
- *Fraud potential.* The company was also often fearful of the following scenario—one that could be avoided simply by asking for that voided check. After setting a vendor up on ACH payment (from a handwritten form with an illegible

signature), the vendor would call and ask why the company had stopped paying them. After further investigation, the staff would discover that the account the company was sending money to did not belong to the company at all, but to a disgruntled mail clerk who had left the company shortly after completing the form with an offshore account set up in an untraceable alias. You should insist on getting a voided check.

- *Vendor setups.* Another mistake was that after going through all this work to clean up vendors, change accounts, and update records, the company did not centralize vendor setups to one individual who was responsible for verifying and maintaining data. It simply changed its procedures to require all new vendors to accept ACH payment in order to be set up in the system, but the procedure was not enforced.

  Vendors that had been blocked for noncompliance were gradually unblocked, and the amount of checks issued began to rise. Without one central department being held accountable for the integrity of the vendor database, the entire effort of the ACH conversion project was completely wasted.

While it is never possible to completely eliminate all problems, using the procedures that follow will make a big dent in the problems you will encounter when starting an ACH payment program—especially if you insist that all your vendors participate:

- Get banking data from a voided check—not a handwritten form.
- Request an up-to-date W-9 at the same time.
- Start your electronic payment program with a small group so you can make adjustments to your program before rolling it out to your entire vendor constituency.
- Before you demand that all vendors accept payments electronically, make sure all your systems and processes are working 100%.

- If one vendor is in your master vendor file more than once, make sure those entries are linked for purposes of updating with banking information.

USE ACH PAYMENTS TO SOLVE THE RUSH CHECK PROBLEM

A rush check (also referred to as an ASAP check) is any check produced outside the normal check production cycle. Organizations that run their checks from a mainframe computer are often forced to either use a typewriter or handwrite a check that is produced outside the normal cycle. Even those that print them on a personal computer have issues with rush checks.

Rush checks not only disrupt the work flow in accounts payable, making the department less efficient, they also open the door to fraud and duplicate payments. An inordinate amount of duplicate payments are checks that were rush checks. This is due to the fact that sometimes the check has been cut and is somewhere in the system, waiting for an approval, a signature, or to be mailed. Inevitably, both checks get cashed—and rarely is the second returned without the prompting of a duplicate payment audit.

The size of the problem will vary at different organizations depending on how good invoice processing procedures are and how accommodating the organization is toward requests for rush checks. Some organizations dig their heels in, issuing rush payments only in cases of dire emergency while others allow them under almost any circumstance.

ACH payments provide a very real solution to the rush check dilemma. By adopting a policy that all rush payments requests that are honored will be fulfilled with an ACH payment, a company solves many of the problems caused by rush checks while simultaneously introducing new vendors to the electronic payment process. The vendor demanding the rush check will have good funds in its account before it would write a check. Often once a vendor experiences the benefits of ACH payments, it will willingly sign up for that type of payment in the future. It can be a win-win for both parties, turning a bad situation into one that improves supplier relations.

Payment Trends

ACH payments are here to stay. The robust consumer acceptance of electronic bill-paying products portends continued B2B growth in this arena.

9

OTHER PAYMENT INITIATIVES

INTRODUCTION

It will come as no surprise to readers that banks have been jumping feet first into the payment arena offering products to help clients with payment issues. As is discussed in Chapter 16, banks were in the lead in developing check fraud protection products, namely positive pay. They also have long been active in the check printing arena, as is discussed in Chapter 15. And they continue to move to develop products to help their customers with their payment issues. In fact, some might claim that the products discussed in this chapter would better belong in Chapter 15 on outsourcing. However, we've decided to keep them separate. While most of this chapter focuses on bank initiatives, we've also included petty cash, as it did not appear to belong anywhere else.

INTEGRATED PAYMENT PRODUCTS

Banks have been on the forefront when it comes to producing payment products. However, they are not alone. Third-party developers have created some pretty nifty models as well. Although a number of stand-alone products address specific issues related to each payment product, products that will handle all payments, regardless of payment methodology, have emerged.

These solutions address all outbound payments, systematically consolidating and integrating most aspects of the payment management process. Typically they allow multiple payment methods. This should including checks, automated clearing house (ACH), and wire transfers. They may also handle purchase cards (p-cards), cash, and stored value cards. If p-cards are included, do not overlook the rebate issue. If the integrated payment product has been purchased from the same organization that issues the p-card, this should not be an issue. If it is a different organization, work with the card issuer on this matter. It should not care how the payment is initiated.

Many integrated payment products provide database functionality, allowing the payment issuer to check on the status of payments, often moments after they have been initiated. Some of the bank products also offer online stop-payment initiation. Additionally, some offer to handle unclaimed property responsibilities.

OTHER FEATURES OF INTEGRATED PAYMENT PRODUCTS

The consolidation of all payment processing into one system is a huge plus. Another bonus is the flexibility to use any number of payment methods. Be aware that, at least currently, the systems do not seem to limit the number of payment types that can be used with each vendor payee. Depending on the other controls built into the process, this may or may not be an issue.

Most bank products integrate into their check clearing process and offer real-time access to the most current information. Thus, when a vendor calls claiming it has not been paid, the accounts payable associate can check online, while the vendor holds on, to see if the check has cleared. If it hasn't, a stop payment could be initiated and a new payment processed without concern for a duplicate payment. Those who use this approach need to check with their bank provider to ensure the timing of each of these transactions. An image of each check is often available on screen within minutes of being paid. This will help determine if fraud is an issue. A quick examination of the image of the back of the check will reveal where it was deposited. Your vendor will know if that is its account or not.

Another nice feature for those who are not currently making electronic payments is that use of one of the integrated systems makes the process of transitioning vendors to this payment type a little easier.

If a centralized database that stores all disbursement details is offered as a feature, it will provide a single interface for all data retrieval, should you choose to purchase that feature. If it is automatically included, you will need to decide whether you want your employees relying on the bank database or your own records when responding to vendor inquiries.

Wire transfers aren't ignored either. To the extent that you are still using wires, the wire transmission process is simplified, and you should automatically receive a confirmation number for each wire sent. Thus, if a vendor calls claiming the wire was not received, you can give it the confirmation number without having to call your bank.

These systems offer flexibility and claim that little or no information technology (IT) involvement is needed to get them up and running. You probably will need to get someone from your IT staff involved, but the time requirement should be a lot less than if you were doing this yourself in-house.

SPECIAL ACH FEATURES

These integrated systems make the transition to ACH a lot easier. For starters, if you use one of these systems, most do not require that you change your existing infrastructure.

Once the ACH has been initiated, the service provider provides confirmation of successful payments and rejection notification with rejection reasons. This allows the payment staff to follow up with the vendor immediately and get corrected information.

To make the reconciliation process easier, some of these products will assign check numbers to ACH payments. Whether this is a good idea or not remains to be seen.

One of the many advantages of ACH payments is the minimization of unclaimed property issues. By following up immediately on all rejected transactions, an organization can effectively eliminate unclaimed property related to ACH transactions. The same cannot be said for checks.

DIFFERENT NOMENCLATURE

We've used the term "integrated payables" to describe the group of products that allow an organization to initiate electronic and check payments by sending a single file of payment instructions to its financial institution. Other terms used to describe this methodology include "e-payables" and "online payables."

Some of the more sophisticated electronic invoicing products on the market today have functionality at the end that permits the creation of a file that can be transmitted to a bank, if that is desired, for the initiation of payments. Alternatively, the organization would use this file to initiate the payments itself.

E-PAYABLES

Before ACH became such a hot payment tool, the best way to get rid of paper and reduce the number of checks issued was to move payments to a p-card. Several financial institutions have products that they refer to as e-payables service, which are designed to replace physical checks with electronic card payments through the global credit card network.

These e-payables products allows organizations to integrate their existing paper check processes and replace the back-end payment with a secure card payment, eliminating costs associated with paper checks and usually earning a rebate in the process. In fact, this rebate often paid for all or part of the costs.

As this market evolves, expect to see more confusion over the terminology and naming of products before it all settles down.

PROCURE-TO-PAY SOLUTIONS

A number of procurement solutions are beginning to incorporate the payment piece into their solution, offering a complete procure-to-pay solution. Typically, these products are accessed on some sort of a portal where the customer can place an order for goods. Depending on how this process is structured, the act of placing an order may generate a purchase order.

When the goods are shipped, an invoice is produced. Again, depending on how the product is structured, the customer either receives the invoice electronically or has to go to the supplier's portal to "pick up the invoice" electronically.

The payment function can be handled in a number of ways. The simplest, but probably least used, is for the supplier to issue an ACH debit against the customer's account based on the prearranged payment terms. This is not likely to be popular in North America. Alternatively, these systems interface with the customers' accounts payable system for the payment piece.

From a payment professional's point of view, this is not really the complete procure-to-pay solution that the developers tout, but it is a giant step in the right direction. Many of the online procurement products initially developed ended at the goods being shipped and a paper invoice being mailed. The last step usually said something like "and then the invoice is paid" without ever explaining how the methodology that would be used to pay the invoice.

In fact, in one project, over $1 million was spent to develop an electronic process without any input about how the payments would be handled. The investment in this supposed completely electronic process had to be scrapped because the second half didn't work. How could it?

There probably will be big improvements in this area in the next few years. Currently many electronic procurement systems and catalogs exist. If payment is electronic, it is often tied to a p-card. This link generally means that the size of each purchase is relatively small. For there to be any true completely electronic procure-to-pay model, there needs to be an integration of all payment types.

In many organizations, the accounts payable staff and the purchasing staff do not always see eye to eye. In fact, that is why the million-dollar project fell apart. No one from the payment side had been included in the development of the complete project. Those organizations that truly want to have a completely electronic procure-to-pay process will have to have purchasing and accounts payable input, and the two groups will have to find ways to work together.

OTHER SMALL-DOLLAR PAYMENTS

Companies that do not have corporate p-cards often find that their petty cash box gets quite a bit of use. This is not good as it is generally considered a best practice to eliminate the petty cash box completely. If that is not possible, organizations are advised to keep reimbursements from the petty cash box to a minimum. Without a corporate-sponsored card, this may be problematic unless an alternative plan is created.

Some organizations encourage their employees to use their own credit cards and then to put in for reimbursement through the organization's travel and entertainment reimbursement process. If the amounts are small enough, employees could use their own cash and apply for reimbursement in a similar manner. Whether this approach is acceptable at an organization will depend largely on its corporate culture.

Employees with credit cards who are interested in earning frequent flyer points associated with the cards generally will not mind using their own cards. However, those without access to credit as well as a few other employees will object. Some are strongly opposed to using a personal card, and you can expect an argument from at least a few on this front. Without a p-card program, it is hard to accommodate the few employees who either can't or won't use their own cards without relying on a petty cash box.

Another alternative is to have a more willing employee make the purchase and put in for reimbursement. Remember this is only for very low-cost items, and it should not happen often.

PayPal

While PayPal is almost exclusively a payment mechanism used by consumers, it has made its impact on the corporate world. Many people, including some of the executives at all organizations, got their first taste of making electronic payments using PayPal to pay for eBay auctions. While this is not a mechanism that would be used by most companies, it did serve to make many more comfortable with the notion of electronic payments. PayPal first started with credit cards but soon moved on to debiting the consumer's bank account with his or her authorization. This is an ACH debit.

Interestingly, a number of smaller organizations that do not have the ability to accept credit cards have started to accept payments via

PayPal. This has happened most commonly with small professional organizations.

Although it is not expected that organizations will use PayPal to make payments, it is worth noting its impact on the electronic payment revolution. PayPal introduced many to the world of electronic payments.

PETTY CASH BOX

Traditionally, companies have utilized petty cash boxes to pay for small-dollar charges that arise in the day-to-day running of the business. Ideally, the box would have a small amount of cash in it and employees would be reimbursed for approved purchases. They would have a receipt of some sort or a form signed by an authorized approver. The petty cash box would be kept locked in a safe. Preferably, the person with the key to the box would be a different individual from the person who knew the combination of the safe.

The opportunity for abuse and outright fraud is huge with petty cash boxes. Phony receipts, questionable accounting, and no real review of the funds spent are just a few of the problems. At a large company, where spending is scrutinized closely, extensive use of petty cash throws the analysis off. One company, after eliminating petty cash, discovered it spent $50,000 a year on pizza for employees working late. Armed with this information, it was able to negotiate a slightly better price on orders.

It is recommended that organizations do not have a petty cash box. They are extremely inefficient and open the door to petty fraud. Given the wide variety of alternatives available today, there is no need for petty cash. Instead, companies can:

- Require that employees use their p-cards or travel and entertainment (T&E) cards to pay for the item in question.
- Pay for the items themselves and put in for reimbursement on their expense reports.

- If a lower-level employee is involved, the department manager can pay for the item and put in for reimbursement on an expense report.
- Have the vendor bill for the item.

If you must have a petty cash box, either for logistical reasons or corporate imperatives, some policies that will help keep the petty cash function under control follow.

- Have a written policy delineating the use of the box.
- Limit the access to the box.
- Keep a log of who goes into the box, the beginning balance, all withdrawals, and the ending balance. Ideally two individuals should verify these items and initial the log.
- Internal audit should perform unscheduled audits of the box.
- Limit the time when the box is open. Don't reimburse employees whenever they show up (unless, of course, it is a true emergency). If possible, open the box only once a week to reimburse employees.
- Whenever a reimbursement is requested, look for other ways to handle the charge. Even if the employee is paid, point out ways the matter could be addressed in the future without resorting to petty cash.
- Never, under any circumstances, take an IOU in the petty cash box.
- Never reimburse an employee who does not have proper documentation and authorization for the expense.
- Replenish the box on a timely basis. Don't allow the box to run low on cash.
- Set stringent checks on who can take money in and out of the box. With several hands in the pot, it can get ugly if money is missing.
- Publish a schedule, along with the requirements, for reimbursement, and share it with all employees likely to use the box.

- Periodically review the expenses reimbursed from the box and look for alternative ways to pay for them.

Payment Trends

There will be continued development of new electronic products that address the payment needs of organizations of all sizes. Financial institutions and third parties will continue to develop payment products that integrate all sorts of payment solutions. The procure-to-pay products on the market will continue to evolve to better include the payment piece and take advantage of all the functionalities available today.

PART THREE

INITIATIVES TO MAKE PAYMENT OPERATION MORE EFFICIENT

Once you have the in-depth knowledge of the current payment arena as well as a thorough understanding of the tools that are available, you will be set to create a payment program that will work for your organization. This part provides the information you need to set up these new programs and then grow them. It's not enough to start a p-card program or e-payments initiative; your staff will need to take the appropriate action to ensure the programs grow. The payment world is definitely not an "if I build it they will come" marketplace.

With your programs in place, you will need to integrate the different programs together to ensure you do not create chaos and that all the programs coexist in peace. Chapter 14 addresses that concern. Chapter 15 takes a look at a topic that is creeping into the B2B environs despite employees' keen attempts to keep it out: outsourcing. It's here, and it's time to look it squarely in the eye and figure out what impact it will have on your organization.

If you've been involved in the payment world at all, then you realize that fraud is an issue that must be dealt with on a regular basis. It not only exists in the paper check world but is slowly finding its way into the electronic payment world, even if you don't make electronic payments. Chapters 16 and 17 are filled with advice on how to combat both types of fraud.

10

STARTING A P-CARD PROGRAM

INTRODUCTION

Once the decision has been made to begin using purchase cards (p-cards), there is a lot of work to be done. If the planning is careful and the groundwork laid cautiously, the program will have a much better chance for success. It will also provide the framework for expansion at a later date. And, as you will see as you read through this book, most organizations that start a p-card program will want to expand it if it is at all successful.

PLANNING STAGE

Begin by vigilantly planning your approach. Start by defining the goals and benefits expected from the program. With this information in hand, there can be no surprises. Once everyone agrees on the goals, it should be fairly easy to set measurable objectives. Without taking these two steps, it will be impossible to say whether the program is a success. If everyone is on the same page, there should be no finger-pointing.

Estimate the potential savings to your organization based on payment volumes and spend. This is crucial to getting the program off the ground. It will provide you with the metric you need to determine if it is worth proposing your program in the first place. Although the numbers will vary from organization to organization, the potential savings has to be significant enough to make the change worthwhile. A $100,000 savings might be worth pursuing for an organization with less than $10 million in annual revenues, but this amount might be insignificant for a Fortune 100 company.

As with any program, senior management support is crucial. Without it, getting the rest of the company behind the program will be difficult. Your p-card program opponents will hinder the implementation every step of the way. As with any new initiative, it is inevitable that there will be those who will look for any excuse not to use the process.

Don't overlook the importance of building interfaces to the general ledger. A significant by-product of the general ledger interface is the population of a database that can be used to promote and control the program.

Develop strategies related to tax, internal audit, purchasing, accounting, and treasury. Do not forget to include representatives from those organizations in the planning stages. Otherwise, an important issue could be overlooked, one that if addressed incorrectly effectively dooms the program.

FINDING A GOOD SERVICE PROVIDER

With planning in place and agreed on, you will need to find a provider. Since you will have to live with whoever is chosen for some time, take time to ensure you select one who will work well with your staff. Ask hard questions of potential p-card providers. Network with other executives who have p-card programs in their organizations to find providers that offer quality service. Ask not only for recommendations but also for horror stories.

Do not overlook asking what your company will have to do to get started. The beginning of any new process is difficult, and you must understand what will be required and that you have adequate staff on hand to handle the initial work. Providers sometimes say that they'll help you but, when push comes to shove, expect to do most of the work yourself.

Contact several card-issuing organizations using either a formal or informal request for proposal (RFP) process. Don't forget to ask for references and to check the references as well. Keep in mind that it is unlikely that a vendor will provide an unhappy reference, but stranger things have happened. In more than one case a card service provider gave the name of a big customer, confident that the reference would not be checked. The provider ended up with egg on their face when the references were verified.

POLICY AND PROCEDURES MANUAL

Like other processes, p-cards need written approved policies and procedures. This is especially important if your program is one where employees who violate program strictures could be subject to immediate dismissal. Without a manual, the manager responsible for the program will have huge headaches.

Since the program is new, organizations have a golden opportunity to "do it right." Not being hampered by existing procedures or established bad habits on the part of card users, managers are in the unique position to get this program off on the right foot.

PILOT PROGRAM

No matter how much planning you do, inevitably there will be an issue you did not anticipate. This could be something that is unique to your company or industry or simply something that fell through the cracks. Therefore, it is strongly recommended that you start with a pilot program. Every project, no matter how well planned or how good the staff is, will have some rough spots in the beginning.

Initial pilot participants should be selected from those who have a need for the card and support the program, not its detractors. There will be time to convert the skeptics later. You do not need them around should the pilot hit some bumps in the road.

Once the pilot program has run for a while and the bumps are worked out, it is time to roll out the program to the rest of the company. By that time your original participants should have done some evangelistic work promoting your program to their peers.

EVALUATING THE PROGRAM

During the planning stage, you set measurable objectives. After a reasonable amount of time, begin to quantify the results. Use this information to determine if you need to tweak the program or if it is getting close to being ready for rollout to a larger audience. Don't forget to get feedback from the p-card users. Often the intelligence you can gather from them will provide insights that you might not have otherwise gotten.

Ask not only how effective they felt the program was but what additional issues need to be addressed. Be sure to give them the opportunity to add unscripted comments. This might include additional areas where the card could be used as well as what might be done to enhance the program. Often input from parties not associated with the process will include an idea that would not have come from traditional sources.

Follow up on the additional issues before the program is rolled out to the general population. You might also start a regular benchmarking program to measure how the program is doing. Revise it as needed.

Do not overlook ongoing communication with the cardholders. This is crucial. It is the only way problems can be identified and corrected before they cause major problems with the p-card program.

MANAGING THE PROGRAM

One of the valued features of p-cards is that they allow the organization to set controls for each employee as needed. At the beginning you might establish card controls for each employee or group of employees as company policy dictates. These can be adjusted as experience is gained, raising certain limits where needed and lowering others.

P-card programs do not operate in a vacuum. It is important to work with the appropriate parties in accounting and information technology (IT) to establish whatever general ledger interface is required. Different companies do it in different ways, depending on corporate preference and the capabilities of the accounting software used.

It is also a good idea to set up a periodic reporting mechanism to keep management apprised of the success of the program. This same reporting can be used to provide others in the company with needed information.

AUDITING THE PROGRAM

Many organizations are concerned about fraud. Others want to ensure that all purchases that should be put on the card are because they want to receive as high a rebate as possible. This is not unusual and is becoming a larger issue.

Thus many organizations will want to set up an audit program to see if p-cards are being used as they should be and in all instances where they are supposed to be.

The purchasing personnel can use the information gathered in these audits to help them negotiate better pricing from preferred vendors. This can be done if all the activity is aggregated to one or two suppliers for large purchases of certain products.

END USER TRAINING

Without adequate training, even the most carefully planned p-card program will have a hard time succeeding. Training is an area that is often overlooked. People think that p-cards are just like credit cards. Because they know how to use credit cards, why do they need special training? Although they are correct that p-cards are similar to credit cards, they are incorrect in the assertion that they do not need any training.

Without training, the cards will be used for items for which they are not intended to be used, reporting and monitoring of spending will be inaccurate, and there will be clashes between the end users and the professionals responsible for monitoring the program.

The best training is on-site in-person instructions on how to use the cards and do the associated reporting. When the program is first rolled out, such training is possible, as usually a large number of employees need to be trained. Unfortunately, on-site in-person training often is not possible for new hires or when employees are located in remote locations and only one or two in each branch use the card.

The next best training is given online, allowing each employee to take the training at his or her convenience. If possible, incorporate online testing to ensure that employees have understood the material.

Some organizations go so far as to refuse to give a p-card to anyone who has not taken the training. As you might expect, you can anticipate some resistance, if not outright rebellion, to the last two recommendations.

ENSURING USAGE

Some organizations have found that after they went through a lot of trouble to set up a program, those who objected to the program simply did not use the cards when issued to them. Such actions could doom an otherwise good program to failure.

If this happens, there are several things you can do. For starters, senior management support is key to enforcing usage in such situations. If the laggards know of management support, they are less likely to play games.

Some organizations return the invoice to the person who should have paid for the item with a note asking that it be paid using the person's p-card. Others take a more stringent approach: They force p-card use by refusing to pay for items not charged to p-cards when applicable.

KEYS TO SUCCESS

You can take 10 steps to make your p-card program a success.

Step 1. *Secure senior management support for the process*. Without it, those who oppose the program will be able to derail the program.

Step 2. *Reengineer current processes*. By making the process more efficient before the p-card is started, inefficient processes aren't proliferated.

Step 3. *Use a pilot model*. A pilot allows for a solid test of the process rather than simply laying it on top of traditional processes.

Step 4. *Dedicate resource, to manage and promote the program*. Do not expect one of your accounts payable staff to run the program off the side of her desk. To make the program successful, dedicated staff must monitor and run the program as well as provide training to potential card users. This training needs to be ongoing; new cardholders will need training before they can begin using their cards and existing cardholders will need to be trained on any modifications that are made.

Step 5. *To get the program started on the right foot, establish a cross-functional team with members from accounting, purchasing, tax, treasury, and internal audit*. This will ensure that all the appropriate issues are addressed in a timely manner.

Step 6. *Establish a clearly defined process and appropriate procedures*. Make sure that the procedures are made readily available to all parties who are affected. This is most easily done by posting on the organization's intranet site. In this manner updates can be posted easily and quickly, and there is no need to send written communications to all affected parties. It also eliminates the possibility that someone who should have been included in the circulation was missed. By putting it on the intranet, anyone who needs to reference the procedures will have ready access.

Step 7. *Set up program goals and metrics that can be substantiated*.

Step 8. *Establish a solid database to control and promote the program*.

Step 9. *Don't underestimate the importance of effective communication throughout the organization*. Make sure everyone who needs information can get it. Periodic, but not too often, e-mail blasts to everyone should make the point.

Step 10. *Communicate your results using metrics*. Make sure you put your results in the language management understands: money. By pointing out savings, you will continue to garner support for the program.

POTENTIAL PROBLEMS

Although p-cards are wonderful, some issues might cause your organization a problem when it comes to getting the program off the ground. By addressing these issues beforehand, your fledgling program will stand the best chance of success. The issues are:

- *Invoice despite a p-card payment.* Some organizations are not able to suppress the printing and mailing of invoices despite having already been paid. Thus, an invoice will arrive for something already paid for with a p-card. Some of these will even be marked (in tiny letters) PAID. Be alert for this to ensure that your organization does not make a duplicate payment, paying once with a p-card and a second time with a check. A best practice to avoid this issue is to limit the payment mechanism for each vendor to one type.
- *1099 obligations remain.* Payments made to independent contractors with p-cards still require that the payor issue a 1099. There has been some talk of the card issuers taking over this responsibility, but as of this writing, that has not occurred. All payments made to independent contractors, regardless of the payment mechanism, require a 1099. If you pay an independent contractor using both a check and a p-card, aggregate the amounts and issue only one 1099.

PAYMENT TREND

As organizations everywhere continue to pursue the rebates aggressively, expect p-card programs to remain and to grow.

11

EXPANDING A P-CARD PROGRAM

INTRODUCTION

As organizations increasingly look for alternatives to the paper check, purchase cards (p-cards) stand out like a shining star when it comes to small-dollar items. Of course, the definition of "small dollars" varies from organization to organization. And as organizations continue to become more enamored with rebates, they are also looking at ways to grow their programs.

INFORMATION TO GROW YOUR PROGRAM

Two organizations work closely with professionals using p-cards: the National Association of Purchasing Card Professionals (NAPCP) and the American Institute of Certified Public Accountants (AICPA) Center for Excellence in Financial Management. The NAPCP is a group of over 700 professionals interested in and responsible for p-cards at their organizations. Whether you are just starting a program or are looking to grow your program, the organization has the resources to help.

The AICPA Center for Excellence in Financial Management decided to investigate p-card use in the financial payment arena. To do so, it funded a survey of companies that use the cards.

AICPA P-CARD SURVEY

The AICPA asked participants about their experiences with the cards and, from that information, identified best practices for p-card use. From this survey, the AICPA concluded that:

- Most companies realized only some of the benefits of p-card use. Thus, there is potential for further expansion at most companies that currently have programs.
- Underachieving programs often were burdened by stringent controls applied to inexpensive items. By taking a realistic look at the controls and loosening them where appropriate, organizations would be able to expand their usage very easily.
- Almost all companies could significantly improve their p-card programs with a few important modifications.

The AICPA says that companies can improve their programs by:

- *Loosening the requirements an employee must satisfy to obtain a p-card.* By making it easier for employees to get cards in the first place, programs could expand easily.
- *Encouraging managers to provide strong support.* As discussed in Chapter 10, strong management support for a program is crucial. Midlevel managers will respond if senior executives strongly back the program. Conversely, if there is no senior-level support for the program, middle managers will rarely go out of their way to encourage usage.
- *Providing information and training to help employees use the cards.* Both up-front and ongoing training is crucial to

the success of p-card programs. The AICPA data backs this assertion.

- *Making it easier to use p-cards.* The AICPA provides this list of ways to make the use easier:
  - Raise spending limits.
  - Broaden spending categories.
  - Reduce restrictions that block the use of certain Standard Industrial Classifications (SIC codes) when submitting expenses.
  - Limit card activity audits.
  - Eliminate logs.
- *Committing resources to promote p-card use.* By assigning responsibility for the p-card program and for its growth to one or more managers, the program stands the best chance of expanding. This responsibility should be separate from other tasks and not something someone with an already overloaded plate is expected to manage.
- *Holding the program administrator responsible for performance targets consistent with p-card spending potential.* This puts pressure on the administrator to make sure others in the company do what they are supposed to do when it comes to using the p-card.
- *Establishing company policies mandating use of p-cards for certain transactions.* In some cases, organizations refuse to pay for goods with a check if a p-card was the intended payment vehicle. Enforcing this policy can lead to a few ugly confrontations until employees get the message that they must use the card; it is not an option.
- *Adopting a "one-card" solution under which p-cards could be used to pay for travel and entertainment.* Don't forget to include fuel as well. One cards are among the best and easiest ways to grow a program.

- *Enhancing back-office technology.* (e.g., automated posting of allocations to general ledger accounts.)

TIPS

As organizations everywhere look to improve the efficiency of their payment programs, p-cards stand out. Not only are they a great way to handle the slew of small-dollar invoices that find their way into every accounts payable department, but use of p-cards helps track spend and monitor compliance. And then of course there is the issue of rebates.

The NAPCP's Lynn Larson is a frequent and popular speaker on p-card topics. She advocates these strategies to help managers who want to expand the use of p-cards within their payment matrix:

Tactic 1. *Combine travel in the program.* A growing number of organizations are taking the one-card approach, incorporating travel into the p-card program. The most popular reason for incorporating travel into the program is to grow the rebate. Since the items are already being paid for with a charge card, it is sometimes easy to adopt this approach.

If you take this approach, carefully analyze the impact on the accounting process as well as on the organization's travel policy.

In addition to the one-card approach already discussed there are also payroll cards and project cards:

- Payroll cards contain an available balance for use and are tied to the actual dollars earned by an employee, such as wages, benefits, or some type of expense reimbursement.
- Project cards are for a specific undertaking. Limits can be set to include a maximum dollar amount and

time limit. Limits can decline as the card is used until time or the credit is depleted.

These p-card variants may not be simple to implement and could require reengineering of processes, personnel, and so forth. Other expansion methods, however, are likely to be easier to implement. It is recommended that professionals pursue the untapped potential within standard p-card programs first.

Tactic 2. *Increase the number of cardholders.* This can be achieved by expanding the program into parts of the organization that currently do not have p-cards. Note that some organizations will be able to increase penetration simply by giving the card to everyone who should have one.

Some firms are overly cautious when issuing cards. A careful study of who is purchasing what sometimes can uncover individuals who have not been included in the program but who should be. But proceed with care—do not overdistribute the cards. It is a fine line to determine exactly when to stop expanding the number of people in the program.

Tactic 3. *Convert more suppliers to p-card payments.* It is recommended that you begin by reviewing company spend data from the accounts payable system for non–p-card vendors to identify supplier opportunities. Once the potential suppliers have been identified, they can be approached.

Determine if the vendors in question already accept credit cards. If so, the task has just gotten a lot simpler. Getting them on the p-card program might be as easy as notifying them that you wish to change your method of payment.

The identified suppliers not currently accepting cards will have to be educated. This is a more difficult task. The education process should be started by explaining the benefits of the program. Tell them how they will benefit.

Tactic 4. *Increase the types of purchases included in the program.* Look at the inventory purchases your company makes. Consider if there is an automated inventory in place. If there is, evaluate how a p-card payment integration would affect the process.

Also look at capital equipment purchases. Make sure you consider that including the p-card may require technology enhancements, such as a new interface to the fixed asset system.

A few companies include large-ticket items, such as utility bills, phone bills, and maintenance agreements. Why? They do this because it impacts the revenue-sharing (rebates) opportunities with the card provider.

A number of companies integrate their e-procurement systems with the p-card. If your company does this, you should consider:

- Type of p-card used (individual, ghost, etc.)
- Integration requirements with the e-procurement system and/or general ledger
- Reconciliation requirements

It is also suggested that meeting expenses, temp labor, some consultants, catering, and training might be able to be paid with a p-card.

When paying the types of expenses just discussed, it is imperative that the company fully evaluate its 1099 reporting process to ensure that it will efficiently pick up the required information.

For temp labor and consultants, some organizations require that the number of hours worked be tracked in a centralized system.

If your company is one such enterprise, this must be considered as well. If you are counting on the Qualified Purchase Card Agent (QPCA) taking care of this issue for you, remember this system has not gone into effect and no effective date has been announced.

When expanding a program, especially when increasing the types of purchases, there may be implications to other departments. They should be included in the planning process. Specifically there may be:

- Accounting implications
- Additional technology requirements
- Interface issues
- Process changes that affect staff
- Data requirements

Before getting started on your expansion plan, remember that there is no one-size-fits-all solution. The suggestions just provided can be used to identify missed opportunities as well as to compose a plan that will work within their own organization's unique constraints. It can be based on several of the methods discussed.

SHARE THE WEALTH

A good deal has been written in this book about rebates. What has not been discussed in any detail is what happens to those rebates. For the most part, they are not included in the organization's budget. Some accounting and accounts payable departments use the rebates to fund items that they could not get budget for. In many instances it is a way of getting technology years before the corporate budgeting process would allow.

Some savvy managers—recognizing that they are not alone when it comes to battling the budget honchos—offer to share the rebate. This is done on a pro-rata basis with departments that spend using the card. Thus it becomes an advantage to use the card. In these instances the fights over using the card end quickly.

CAVEAT

With all the talk about expanding the program, we sometimes lose sight of the fact that occasionally cards have to be canceled. The most obvious instance is when an employee leaves the company. Make sure to institute card cancellation procedures.

These procedures put everyone on notice that the card can be revoked at any time the corporation sees fit. This is especially important in the case of employee termination. Regardless of the reason, when an employee leaves, the manager should have the ability to cancel the card immediately—even if the parting is amicable or the employee leaves on his or her own volition. Not canceling a card under these circumstances is begging for trouble. Most card issuers will be able to handle this requirement.

Payment Trend

P-card expansion is possible, especially if some of the simple issues identified are used. With corporate pressure on, it is likely that these tips will turn out to be real winners for those charged with growing their programs.

12

STARTING AN E-PAYMENT PROGRAM

INTRODUCTION

Even if you haven't already begun an electronic payment program and aren't planning a rollout, you should probably begin at least to learn the basics. The benefits are numerous, and many suppliers are clamoring to be paid electronically. It's not a case of *if* you are going to pay electronically but *when*. More than one manager has had to eat his we'll-never-pay-that-way words when a key supplier demanded to be paid electronically as part of the contract. What's more, a few suppliers are offering a small discount, similar to early pay discounts, to those customers who pay electronically. When you do the math associated with even the tiniest of discounts on large expenditures, the rationale for such a program is hard to refute.

BACKGROUND

The Automated Clearing House (ACH) Network is a nationwide batch-oriented electronic funds transfer system governed by the National Automated Clearing House Association (NACHA) Operating Rules, which provide for the interbank clearing of electronic payments for participating depository financial institutions. The Federal Reserve and Electronic Payments Network act as ACH operators, central clearing facilities through which financial institutions transmit or receive ACH entries.

ACH payments include:

- Direct deposit of payroll, Social Security and other government benefits, and tax refunds (some organizations also use this for reimbursement of travel and entertainment [T&E])
- Direct payment of consumer bills such as mortgages, loans, utility bills, and insurance premiums
- Business-to-business payments
- E-checks
- E-commerce payments
- Federal, state, and local tax payments

Nearly 14 billion ACH payments were made in 2005, a 16.2% increase over 2004, according to statistics compiled by NACHA—the Electronic Payments Association. Annual ACH payment volume has doubled in the last five years, spurred by growth across all transaction categories.

HOW PROGRAMS GET STARTED

New payment programs will be started for any one of these reasons:

- Someone in accounts payable or treasury recommends the vehicle. It can take several go-rounds before approval to start is received.

- Someone in management hears a talk on the benefits and comes back and orders accounts payable to start paying all vendors electronically.
- A key supplier asks your organization to pay it electronically.
- A key supplier demands you pay electronically if you want to continue buying from the company.

BENEFITS

The advantages of electronic payments are numerous. Lower cost typically heads the list of reasons organizations make the move. ACH payments are estimated to cost about 10 cents apiece while checks can range in cost from $3 to $20, depending on the process and efficiency of the issuing organization. Additional advantages include:

- Elimination of mailing costs.
- Supplier convenience through eliminating the check-cashing function.
- Simpler cash application process for the vendor when an e-mail with the pertinent details is sent along with the payment.
- No uncashed checks means escheat issues are eliminated.
- Exception handling is minimized as errors are reduced.
- Accounting issues are also reduced.

THE FIRST STEP

As with any high-level project, management buy-in is essential. Without management support, your program will fall apart as the complainers in your organization start whining. Even better than management support is a management evangelist, who fervently backs the program.

The cost savings associated with a program is a good way to get management support, as any savings offered by vendors for paying electronically go right to the bottom line. In fact, some organizations have used the program (at least initially) as a vendor benefit and asked for small discounts as a reward for paying electronically. Whether you will be able to do this will depend in large part on whether it is standard in your industry.

If you can't get support for the program, wait for the right opportunity. This might be when management calls for downsizing. Another opportunity might arise when a problem crops up that would not have occurred if you had the program in place.

It is also a good idea to make your bank your partner in this endeavor. As you launch the program, you will depend on the bank a great deal. Don't overlook this valuable resource.

Get input for your program from all affected parties, including likely critics. If you include them up front, they are less likely to cause problems down the road. In fact, if they feel they are part of the program, they may even advocate for it among other complainers.

Realize that it will be necessary to spend quite a bit of time coordinating the program at the start. Make a realistic assessment regarding information technology (IT) resources. Do you have the capability in-house, or will it be necessary to hire an outside service to get your program up and running? Even if the resources are available in house, will you be able to get an adequate allocation? What's more, if you get the allocation, do you expect the IT staff to be pulled off your project as more pressing projects arise?

Don't underestimate the effect instituting electronic payments will have on your staff. Getting vendors up and running takes time. Don't try to convert all your suppliers at once. Carefully estimate just how many vendors can be converted at one time. Better to have too few candidates in your first offering than too many.

Develop policies and procedures on how to make electronic payments from the accounts payable department. Make sure these processes are integrated into your entire payment process. This will mean involving purchasing and other accounting units. Some adjustments may have to be made in the accounting software to ensure that purchase orders (POs) are canceled and checks are not cut when the payment is initiated.

A GOOD STARTING POINT

It's best to iron out the kinks in-house before testing the process on valued suppliers. You might require all payments to employees be made using the ACH. Be aware that while it is possible to do this for T&E reimbursements, some states do not allow organizations to mandate electronic payments for paychecks. Make sure to check your state requirements before trying this with payroll.

Perhaps some of your employees have been asking to be reimbursed electronically. If you want to start with a very small group to ensure the program is working, ask them to be your beta candidates.

To reduce calls from vendors or employees who don't know what the payments are for or don't realize they received them, provide e-mail notification capability, which may be linked to the vendor master file. This will mean getting e-mail addresses and keeping that file updated.

THIRD-PARTY PARTICIPATION

When you are ready to invite participation, review your vendor listings. You might begin with those suppliers who have requested electronic payment in the past. You won't have to hold their hands as you walk them through the process. In fact, they may offer you some tips.

You might also consider those suppliers already being paid by wire transfer. They are accustomed to electronic payments, and the switch from wire to ACH will save your firm from paying wire transfer fees. Some organizations initiate wires outside the accounts payable process. Depending on your accounting system, ACH may tighten controls as all payments will go through one process instead of two.

When you are confident that you have everything under control, turn your attention to your suppliers. Once you are satisfied with the retooled program, roll it out to a small group. Get feedback again, and if necessary tweak the program to meet any objections and suggestions.

Make it easy for them to sign up. Send a letter to your targeted vendors including an ACH authorization form. Once again, start with a targeted list. The reason for this is simple: The response rate might be higher than you expect. If discounts are available from vendors for electronic payments, you will want to work with purchasing to ensure that you receive all you can.

REPLACING WIRE TRANSFERS WITH ACH PAYMENTS

For organizations that pay many obligations with wire transfers, the ACH alternative will save them a bit of money. This savings is often an added incentive to start such a program. Should you decide to replace wires with ACH, do not overlook the issue of availability of funds. Discuss it with each payee if you think it will be an issue. Most wires result in funds being available immediately, on the day the of wire, for the recipient.

If you use the ACH, typically the funds are available the following day, although they should post on the day the ACH is done. This is similar to a check that might be deposited on one day but not be good funds for two or three days. If this timing is important, say in the payoff of a loan, you might have to initiate the ACH a day or two earlier. However, if the only concern is the date the funds hit the recipient's account, then there is no issue.

BEFORE ROLLING OUT TO YOUR ENTIRE LIST

Once you have a number of vendors enrolled, take a step back. Don't assume everything is going well; inquire if it is. Send an e-mail with your name and phone number to vendors included in the program. It is important to identify potential problems early in the game, when it is easier to fix them and not too many potential payees have been turned off by your process.

You should also anticipate problems. Talk to your peers at other companies and see what their experiences were. Here's a list of some problems encountered by professionals with active programs:

- Incorrect bank account information from suppliers
- Input errors
- Bank mergers resulting in changes to a bank's routing number
- Vendors failing to notify customers when closing or changing bank accounts
- ACH kickback notices not received
- Vendors not receiving e-mails with payment information

VENDOR PARTICIPATION

Identify what payments you want to include. If there is any chance that you will want to pay someone at some point with a purchase card (p-card), do not invite the vendor to participate in your electronic payment program. Here's why. When vendors receive a payment via p-cards, they must pay the bank a processing fee. This typically is between 2 and 3% unless the vendor is very small, in which case it might be higher.

Vendors that receive payments electronically will be extremely reluctant to accept credit card payments in lieu of electronic payments. Once this bell is rung, it is almost impossible to unring it. The only possible exception would be for very small payments, for which p-cards are ideal.

Break your target vendor list down into where you want to start and those payments and vendors who you might eventually want to include once the program is successful. Be aware that as word spreads, you may get requests to join your program. Remember also that if you are going to ask for a pricing discount, a small rebate, or renegotiated payment terms, you will need to include purchasing, if that is the department that negotiates such issues with suppliers. This is a good way to improve relations with purchasing if they are frayed.

Also, once you get started, you may find that vendors who did not initially want to participate in your program will change their minds. Alternatively, another customer may have demanded they accept payments electronically and once they started, they find they prefer payments in this manner.

Be careful how you roll out your e-payment program. If you try to enroll too many vendors in at once, the program may blow up as you don't have adequate staff to handle it.

DOCUMENT, DOCUMENT, DOCUMENT

When you introduce an e-payment program, your procedures will change. Update your policies and procedures manual, and share this information with all affected parties. If you have your procedures posted on your intranet site, add the new e-payment processes.

Not only will you have to write new procedures for the e-payment program, you may have to revise other sections that are affected by your new process. Do not overlook these.

This might also be a good time to review some of your forms used in the payment process and bring them up-to-date.

TRAIN, TRAIN, TRAIN

With your new procedures in place, you will need to make sure the entire staff knows the new process. Never assume that the information is too basic. The accounts payable staff as well as anyone affected by the process, perhaps including purchasing and suppliers enrolled in the program, will need some training.

Without training, you could doom the program. Should one vendor have a bad experience, even if it was entirely the vendor's fault, you will have a hard time convincing that company to continue to participate in your program.

Once the program is up and running and you are ready to invite every vendor to participate, include an e-payment enrollment form with your new vendor pack and a welcome letter. Do not forget to ask for a voided check so you can verify the account number as well as the transit and routing numbers. Your vendor may offer a deposit ticket instead of the voided check. This will work most of the time. However, a few banks do not include the requisite information on their deposit tickets. Thus, if at all possible, get the voided check.

DON'T OVERLOOK METRICS

Most organizations adopt an e-payment program at least partially because of the cost savings associated with the process. Having promised management certain savings, it's a good idea to go back periodically and measure those savings to make sure the program is producing. It is also a good idea to do this so the next time you make a proposal and are asked about the savings related to e-payments, you will not be blindsided.

The savings are not always that easy to quantify. At a minimum, they should include:

- Postage savings of not having to mail checks
- Check printing costs
- Check clearing costs at the bank
- Any discounts or rebates received from vendors for paying electronically
- Any headcount reductions that may occur as a result
- Time savings resulting from not having to process checks

Other savings may be unique to your organization. Include them. Of course, since you are including all the check-related costs, you will need to offset your savings with the cost the bank charges you for ACH payments.

VENDOR SATISFACTION SURVEY

Periodically, perhaps as part of a larger vendor satisfaction survey, ask participants in your program about their experiences. Take the results seriously, and tweak your program if the survey results indicate a weakness in your approach. Do not overlook the opportunity to ask participants for suggestions.

It is hoped that they will share with you approaches taken by other companies that work well—techniques you can incorporate into your own program. Use the survey to learn from your own mistakes as well as the success of others. There is absolutely no reason why if you see a good idea at another company you cannot bring it home and make it your own.

PAYMENT TREND

According to a recent *Accounts Payable Now & Tomorrow* survey, 73% of all organizations now make at least a few ACH payments. This is up drastically from 34% five years ago. Of the participants, 91% said they expected to be making payments through the ACH within five years. The number is probably understated. If you do not currently have an ACH program, begin investigating one. It's only a matter of time before the market will require it of you.

13

EXPANDING AN E-PAYMENT PROGRAM

INTRODUCTION

You're convinced and you've even managed to get management on board. You all agree that paying electronically makes a lot of sense—both for you and for the suppliers you pay. Having won the internal battle, you now face your next challenge: getting an appropriate level of participation in the program. Not only does the program make financial sense for the company, but you've put your reputation on the line. How are you going to deliver?

MARKET STATUS

E-payments alleviate many of the problems associated with paper checks. They are among the most cost-efficient payment mechanisms currently available. This is one of those issues that is actually win-win for both parties. Unlike other matters in business, where one party gains at the expense of the other, the automated clearing house (ACH) payment mechanism really does benefit both parties.

A few savvy vendors in aggressive markets will use ACH to develop a competitive advantage for their products. They do this in several ways. One technique currently in use is to offer slight pricing discounts or rebates to those customers who agree to pay them electronically. In cutthroat markets, this could give one supplier an advantage over another.

Another technique used is to renegotiate payment terms to make the transaction float neutral. Until recently, the request for the renegotiated payment terms came almost entirely from the customer. Now, in an attempt to entice participation, a few vendors are voluntarily offering slightly extended terms.

Don't think that because the vendor hasn't offered the pricing discount or renegotiated payment terms, they aren't available. Ask. Often vendors will grant them if asked; if not asked, however, they stay mum on the subject.

TECHNIQUES TO GROW YOUR E-PAYMENT PROGRAM

Some strategies to raise supplier participation in your program follow.

- *Don't bite off more than you can chew.* Begin by figuring out how many suppliers you could comfortably convert from paper to electronic payment in a given month. There is a good reason to do this. If the response to your first offering is overwhelming, you may not be able to process in a timely manner everyone who expresses interest. The worst thing you could do for your new electronic initiative is not deliver. If you fail with a particular supplier the first time out, it is going to be a long time before you get that supplier's agreement again.
- *Start slow with a test group.* These should be suppliers that either are already accepting payments electronically and/or those with whom you have a really good relationship—those vendors that won't be turned off if the first pass doesn't go as smoothly as you'd like. Vendors that have solicited

you to pay them electronically make excellent candidates for your test group. Since they've requested you pay them electronically, they are more likely to be understanding if things go awry in the beginning.

- *Roll out your program.* Once you've figured out what you can reasonably handle and your processes are working smoothly, send out a mass mailing to targeted suppliers you want to pay electronically. You might, for example, exclude those suppliers you prefer to pay using the purchase card (p-card). Not everyone you solicit will accept your electronic invitation. So, if you can handle 100 conversions a month, send your initial solicitation to 200 or 300. Keep running your monthly solicitations until you have gone through your entire targeted market.
- *Get on the phone.* Once you've finished your initial campaign, you are ready to take the next, more aggressive, step. You'll need to go after the laggards who did not have the good sense to sign up for your electronic payment initiative. Begin by outlining all the benefits of receiving payments electronically. Once you have the list firmly in hand, pick up the phone and start calling. Sometimes all it takes is a simple phone call and a little conversation to get the ball rolling. At other times, the vendor will have a real objection, a reason electronic payments cannot be accepted. Address these issues if you can. If you can't, note what they are for future reference.
- *If you can't get in the front door, try climbing in through a window.* Now you have to get sneaky. The next time one of your nonparticipating vendors calls looking for a payment that was needed yesterday, take advantage of the opportunity. Even if the delay is entirely your company's fault, suggest that you can pay electronically today or tomorrow (whatever your schedule allows) but will not be able to draw a check and mail it until.... Point out that given mail time, it might

take a week or more until the vendor has the funds in its account, but if you pay electronically, it can have good funds the next day.

- *The door is never completely closed.* After six months or even perhaps a year, revisit the issue with those who have not signed up. More often than not you will find that a vendor who did not have the capability when it was first suggested has upgraded, and you will be able to enroll a portion of this group.
- *Roll up your sleeves and get ready to work.* Now it's time to address the "problem children," the companies that have real operational issues that prevent them from accepting electronic payments. Go back to the notes you took when making your initial phone calls. Categorize them and identify the most common issues. Then look for solutions to those problems. See if any of the vendors you are currently paying electronically had these issues. If they did, find out how they solved the problem. Armed with this information, you are prepared to provide your suppliers with a potential solution. If the solutions you offer have some value, you may not only add the vendor to your electronic payment clients, but you will also have enhanced the relationship with that vendor—something purchasing should appreciate!
- *Take a real hard-ball approach.* This tactic won't work in every situation (especially if you are dealing with some 800-pound gorilla suppliers), but it will work on occasion. Levy a fee on those vendors who refuse to be paid electronically. Charge them $25 for every check you cut to them. (Note: Depending on the relationship you are trying to foster with your suppliers, this may not be a tactic you and your firm chose to employ. Accounts payable professionals should do this only with management's blessing and purchasing's knowledge. Should a key vendor complain, or, worse, halt

This is the best of all worlds for customers. They get to pay with the least expensive payment mechanism while simultaneously getting a price reduction or rebate—both of which effectively increase the bottom line. The offer of such savings has been more than enough to convince quite a few organizations to convert to electronic payments.

Like discounts offered for early payments, these incentives should be viewed positively and taken if at all feasible, assuming, of course, that they make financial sense.

IMPROVED TERMS VERSUS PRICING DISCOUNTS

Generally speaking, the improved payment terms offered to make a transaction float neutral translates into two or three days added to the terms. Occasionally, if a vendor is very interested in getting paid electronically, it might offer an additional five days to make the transaction float neutral.

Pricing discounts, however, will generally be some fraction of 1%. Again, this is not a huge amount, unless you are talking about large invoices. However, it is found money that goes straight to the bottom line.

Although you should do the math if you are doubtful, generally speaking, pricing discounts or rebates should be taken, if offered, before the slightly extended payment terms.

If approaching the vendor to ask for an incentive, start with the pricing discount and then move on to the renegotiated terms to make the transaction float neutral.

UNIVERSAL PAYMENT IDENTIFICATION CODE

Even in this day and age, you will occasionally run into vendors who refuse to give you their bank account numbers so you can pay them electronically. They say they are concerned about their banking information being used fraudulently. Given the general concern about sharing banking information, it became apparent awhile back that a universal intermediary was needed. This was the genesis of UPIC.

A UPIC is a banking address used to receive electronic credit payments. A UPIC acts exactly like a bank account number; however, the UPIC protects sensitive banking information, that is, the bank account number and the bank's routing/transit number. The UPIC masks these numbers. Only credits to an account can be initiated with a UPIC. All debits are blocked, increasing security and control. Thus, a crook could not issue an ACH debit, write a check, or issue a demand draft.

If you are wondering if the UPIC can be used with wire transfers, the answer, at least for the present, is no. Initially the UPIC may be used only in place of ACH credits.

Getting Started

If your vendors need instructions on how to get started, direct them to their bank. UPICs can be obtained from a participating bank. Most major banks will be able to facilitate this transaction. Contact your customer relationship manager or branch manager to find out if the bank issues UPICs.

It does not take long for the UPIC to be activated. Generally 24 hours after the application, the number will be live. It should be communicated with the universal routing and transit number (URT) for the bank. To be certain your vendor gets this right, the bank providing the UPIC should verify the URT.

Benefits

Should your customers still be dragging those proverbial feet, you can point out some of these advantages. UPICs:

- Eliminate the risk of lost or damaged checks sent in the mail.
- Increase cash flow as they will receive funds faster, generally on settlement day.

- Eliminate nonsufficient funds (NSF) checks and the worry about checks bouncing.
- Reduce processing costs as ACHs costs next to nothing to receive.
- Gain efficiencies because fewer hands touch the payment, reducing headcount.
- Lower banking fees, as there is no need for lockbox and other check services.
- Enable automatic reconciliation as receiving electronic payments is the first step toward attaining straight-through processing.

Moving Forward

Once a company has obtained a UPIC, it can take aggressive action to solicit electronic payments. Some experts recommend that companies include their UPIC, along with the UTR, on their invoices much in the same way as some forward-thinking companies include their tax identification number (TIN).

Accounts payable professionals who process invoices should be alert to see if any of their vendors have taken that step. This will alert you to another candidate for an electronic payment program.

Even if your firm is not currently making payments electronically, it will probably start at some point, probably in the near future. You might keep a list of your vendors with UPICs on their invoices. Then, when you are looking for test vendors to start paying electronically, you won't have to look far.

Payment Trend

Use of ACH payments will continue to expand due to cost savings and vendor demand. Rebates, pricing discounts, and renegotiated payment terms will become more common as organizations that are offered them by one vendor request them from others.

14

INTEGRATED PAYMENT PROGRAM

INTRODUCTION

The array of payment options available today can be confusing. No longer is it automatic that an organization receives an invoice and a check is written. Firms that are savvy about the payment process are setting up integrated programs that match the payment vehicle to the supplier, choosing the one that is most appropriate for each. Rather than run out and start using all the vehicles available, care should be taken to ensure that each is done correctly and doesn't result in vendor dissatisfaction and duplicate payments.

Start new programs one at a time. If you are starting a purchase-card (p-card) program, consider waiting until that program is up and running before starting your e-payment program. Resources are generally limited in the business world, so allocate them wisely and don't spread them too thin.

There is another fact that bears discussing. When starting any new program, your operation will get worse before it gets better as the kinks get ironed out. This is inevitable. No matter how carefully you plan, there's always an unforeseen issue or circumstance. Sometimes they are related to special industry requirements; other times they occur because of corporate culture strictures. Don't give up. Once you have worked out the curveballs in your programs, the payment process will be more efficient.

WHY NOT STICK WITH CHECKS?

By now you may be thinking, "This is too complicated. We'll just stay with checks for payments." All invoices and payments are not created equal. One of the goals of a well-run payment program is to focus attention appropriately. This means that more attention gets focused on higher-dollar items. You can achieve this by finding ways to process low-dollar items efficiently without opening the door to fraud and duplicate payments. That's where p-cards come in.

Another goal for many organizations is to keep costs down. This translates into controls on headcounts. For many companies, the move to one of the payment alternatives came as a result of mandatory headcount reductions. When required to reduce staff, companies look for ways to handle the same work with fewer people. That's why many adopted both p-cards and automated clearing house (ACH) payments.

And finally, there are those people who look ahead and realize that they can either drive the change in their organization or they can wait for that change to drive them. The shrewd ones decide to get into the driver's seat.

SAMPLE PROGRAM

For most organizations, their payment program simply evolved, with most payments being made by paper check. This situation is gradually changing, given the efficiency savings associated with p-cards and direct demand payments. Organizations that adopted these techniques usually have done so to gain process improvements and cost reductions. Rarely has an organization stepped back, reviewed its payments, and set up a program that combines all payment types, with different types used according to what is deemed appropriate.

For example, an organization might create this type of payment plan:

- P-cards for purchases under $1,000, where cards are taken
- Direct payments (ACH credits) for all vendors converted to the plan who do not take p-cards
- Direct payments (ACH debits) for sales and use tax
- Wire transfers for all real estate transactions
- Travel and entertainment (T&E) reimbursed by ACH credits only
- Checks for everything else
- No invoices process under $10

  If the vendor does not take p-cards, the employee should pay for it him- or herself and request reimbursement through the T&E process.

Yes, petty cash is an option that some organizations still use. Since it is generally an inefficient practice, it is not included in the hypothetical plan discussed here. But, depending on your circumstances, it might be included in your plan.

Given the advances in the payment arena, organizations are starting to evaluate their payment practices and determine where they want to go.

GETTING STARTED

If you have not evaluated your payment practices in a long time, perhaps it is time to start. Begin by running some metrics. Your information technology (IT) department should be able to get the following information for you. Figure out how many payments you have made in the last 18 to 24 months, month by month. These data should be further broken down to determine the total spend and number of payments at different levels (i.e., under $100, how many under $500, under $1,000, under $10,000, under $50,000, etc.).

The dollar levels selected will be what you feel is appropriate for your organization and will depend on your business and your corporate culture. You can use this information to make the case for the strategies you will recommend as well as signature levels for your checks.

At the same time, review the various payment options (check, wire, direct payment, p-card, and T&E reimbursement). Do some research as to what is required for each of the options. Reading this book is a good start. In devising your plan, consider what limitations your systems and corporate culture might play in your proposal.

For example, some companies don't have a p-card program and management is reluctant to approve one. So, p-cards might not be part of your final recipe. Along the same lines, if you would like to push for direct payments for most payments but management is unlikely to back a strong-arm approach requiring vendors to accept payments electronically, it might not be wise to plan for 50% participation in that initiative.

ESTABLISHING THE PLAN

Once you feel you have a good idea, begin by marking out where you currently are regarding payments. For most companies, it might be something like 25% p-cards, 60% checks, 13% direct payments, and 2% wire transfers. Then decide where you'd like to be in three years, taking reality into account. With these two numbers, you can begin to devise an action plan that will get your payment program to where you want to be.

Rome wasn't built in a day and neither will your new and enhanced payment program. Chapters 10 and 12 spelled out for you how to roll out new p-card and electronic payment programs while Chapters 11 and 13 spelled out how you could expand these programs. The processes described in these chapters can be integrated into your overall payment program.

The best of these plans will incorporate several of the payment vehicles, utilizing the best approach for each type of payment you may have.

OTHER FACTORS TO CONSIDER

Do not assume that the processes that worked in the check world will automatically work for your new payment mechanism. While the accounts payable department is pretty good at addressing these issues, the new payment mechanisms are increasingly being used by individuals who work in other departments. Some of these people are not as aware of these issues as they should be. It is imperative that anyone who initiates a payment, regardless of the mechanism used, understands the issues and addresses them appropriately. Here are some issues you might want to evaluate as you set up your new payment process:

- W-9 must be requested, regardless of who initiates payment or payment type. This includes payments made on p-cards. There is some talk of having the card issuer take over this responsibility, but to date that has not happened.
- If several different payment types are used, they need to be aggregated when producing the 1099 for independent contractors.
- Ideally, the system should be set up so that for each vendor, only one payment type could be used. This would alleviate the 1099 aggregation issue.
- The three-way match should be done even if payment is made outside accounts payable. Obviously, this issue goes away if payment is made by p-card at the point of purchase.

- Purchase orders should be canceled when the payment is made regardless of where payment is initiated.
- Invoice numbers can be accessed regardless of who initiates payment and what type of payment it is. This is crucial when checking for duplicate payments before the payment is made.
- Everyone who makes payments, regardless of type, uses the same coding standards for:
  - Vendor name
  - Invoice number
  - Invoice number creation for invoices without invoice numbers

STATEMENTS

Statements have their place in the payment world. With one exception they should not be used to initiate a payment. It is generally an accepted practice that accounts payable requests statements with all activity from all vendors at least once a year, if not once a quarter.

The main purpose of these requests is to identify credit balances that the organization is not aware it has coming to them. The statements can also be used to identify invoices submitted for payment but lost somewhere. Organizations are cautioned against paying from statements, as this can lead to duplicate payments.

There is one time when statements may be used to initiate payment. In cases where a firm receives many small-dollar invoices, processing can clog accounts payable, taking valuable time away from the handling of high-dollar invoices. If a vendor (such as overnight delivery services and temporary employment firms) submits many such invoices, a change in process may work. Instead of paying each individual invoice, you might pay from statements once a week or once a month. Should you decide to take that approach, you must integrate a few steps into your process. Specifically:

- The vendor must agree to this approach.

- Your system must be changed so that invoices will not be paid.
- The system should be modified so that only invoices or only statements can be processed for each vendor.
- Appropriate verifications should be incorporated into the process.

While this is a great way to get rid of numerous small-dollar invoices, care must be taken to ensure that invoices are not inadvertently paid twice. This means the vendor has to have an efficient method to identify invoices paid with each statement. Otherwise, you will have an invoice included twice and therefore paid twice.

WAYS TO HANDLE SMALL-DOLLAR ITEMS EFFICIENTLY

Allocating time efficiently is always a challenge when you have more tasks than resources to handle them. For accounts payable, one of the best ways to address this issue is to find a way to handle small-dollar invoices efficiently. A few ways you can accomplish that include:

- Pay with p-cards.
- Pay from statements.
- Have the employee pay for the item and request reimbursement through the T&E process.
- Pay out of the petty cash box, if you have one (not recommended; but a practical approach if small payments are extremely rare).
- Pay by e-payments (ACH).
- Pay using assumed receipt/negative assurance.

ASSUMED RECEIPT/NEGATIVE ASSURANCE

The three-way match has been mentioned several times. While it is an important technique, it takes time. Thus, for small-dollar invoices, some accounts payable organizations have turned to a different approach.

When accounts payable receives an invoice, it assumes that the goods have been received. Rather than go through the tedious three-way matching process, the department processes the invoice for payment, with only a notification to the person who ordered the goods.

Some also call the approach "negative assurance" because copies of the invoices are sent to the appropriate party. If that individual does not tell accounts payable not to pay, the payment goes out as scheduled. Some innovative companies are beginning to send the notification by e-mail rather than sending copies of the invoice. This approach may seem new to many, but some companies have used the process for several years. This technique is also sometimes referred to as positive receiving.

HOW ORGANIZATIONS PREVENT DUPLICATE PAYMENTS

Duplicate payments continue to be a serious problem in the corporate world. As organizations move toward multiple payment mechanisms, care needs to be taken that they do not inadvertently increase the problems. Duplicate payments are a thorn in the side of most financially savvy managers, who recognize that strong internal controls play a large role in minimizing the impact of the problem.

Data

Accounts Payable Now & Tomorrow recently surveyed its readers, asking them to identify all the techniques they use to prevent duplicate payments. Participants were instructed to check all techniques used. A list of the most common techniques along with the percent of respondents utilizing each follows.

- Coding standards for invoices: 26.17%

- Controls on the master vendor file: 20.81%
- Coding standards on the master vendor file: 15.44%
- Double-check all large items before payment is released: 12.08%
- Run duplicate payment checking routines before checks are released: 10.07%
- Third-party duplicate payment audit firms: 9.40%
- Other 6.04%

Analysis of the Responses

As you can see, the three most popular techniques revolve around good internal controls and processes. Strong appropriate processes in this area will eliminate some of the duplicate payment problem by not allowing a second invoice to slip through under the guise of being a different invoice. The controls on the master vendor file will also help with fraud issues.

No matter how good your processes are, they never completely eliminate the problem. There are numerous reasons for this. Vendors who send a second invoice often add one digit to the original invoice number. While this may help vendors with their accounting, it wreaks havoc with duplicate payment checking routines that focus on the invoice number, as most do. And as most readers are painfully aware, disputes lead to delayed payments as both parties work to get them resolved. This delay often leads to that dreaded second or even third invoice, which more than occasionally gets paid.

These are just a few of the reasons duplicate payments get made, despite good up-front controls. We haven't discussed poor invoice processing systems and fraud. Our discussion was merely to demonstrate how duplicate payments get made, even when there are good controls in accounts payable.

Thus, we believe that after-the-fact checking is crucial. Some organizations set up their own duplicate payment audit group, professionals who do nothing but audit payments after the fact. They also recover duplicate pays for their organization. However, most accounts payable departments do not have the luxury of having staff to assign to this chore. Those who recognize the importance of this process bring in a third-party auditor. Some of the many good reasons to do this include:

- Most work on a contingency basis so it is not necessary to have a budget allocation to do this.
- It's always a good idea to have a second (or third) set of eyes looking at the same transaction.
- Duplicate payments are made by virtually every organization (93% of those participating in the survey revealed that they had at least one check returned by a vendor as a duplicate).
- Since funds recovered are generally not included in an organization's budget, many use the money to pay for a project or equipment that might not get a budget allocation for under different circumstances.

In fact, some organizations have a primary and then a secondary audit done by two different firms. Others have the first audit done by in-house staff, as described, and then use a third-party firm for the secondary audit.

Other techniques used to prevent duplicate payments include:

- Look at duplicate payment amounts each period.
- Establish a policy on entering invoices.
- Perform an internal audit review.
- Apply statistical analysis (outliers, Benford analysis, payment scatter analysis, etc.).
- Use a software system that, with the accounts payable department, "rules" on how to key invoice numbers and set up vendor IDs.
- The computer checks for duplicate invoices when entering the invoices for payment.
- PeopleSoft software allows duplicate controls when vouchers are entered.

- The system does not allow duplicate invoices.
- Issue one purchase order for almost all purchases.
- Have the accounts payable system warn if invoice has been used for this vendor before. The system will not allow the entry if it also has the same date.

Use these techniques described. Not only will they help reduce the payments, they make good sense and will help demonstrate strong internal controls for your Sarbanes-Oxley audit. Should you not be using a third-party audit firm at this time, seriously consider having an audit done for the last two years' activity.

MULTIPLE MECHANISMS AND DUPLICATE PAYMENTS

Special care must be taken when setting up new payment mechanisms to ensure that invoices are not paid twice. That is why it is recommended that organizations limit each supplier to one payment type. Special care should be taken if p-cards are used at the point of sale. Some vendors say that they cannot get their systems to suppress the printing and mailing of invoices, even if a credit card has been used. These invoices have been a cause of duplicate payments. Although some are marked paid or zero balance owing, not all do so. Some vendors still send invoices.

Whether the invoice shows the p-card payment or not, these invoices get paid more than occasionally. Any time more than one payment vehicle is used, the procedures need to be updated to ensure that payments cannot be made using two vehicles, as in the p-card example above.

Payment Trends

As we move forward, organizations will pay their bills using a combination of tools. As you create your program, it is imperative to integrate appropriate internal controls and segregation of duties to ensure that duplicate payments are not made and that fraud opportunities are minimized, if not eliminated.

15

Outsourcing

INTRODUCTION

For years most employees considered even the mention of outsourcing as a taboo subject. Yet, slowly, with the ever-increasing emphasis on cost control and bottom-line accountability, outsourcing of certain functions became semiacceptable. Few organizations today don't outsource some or most of their payroll functionality. Yet when it comes to payment and related functions, the move toward outsourcing has occurred less frequently.

P-CARDS

Background

Rarely is the entire payment function outsourced, although a few organizations have taken that step. Rather, the move has come on the task level. Very gradually, certain specialty functions were outsourced. The function most closely related to payments that is outsourced is check printing. Quite a number of organizations will handle the entire invoice processing and payment initiation functionality in their own shop. They will then create a check issuance file, which will be sent to their banks for check printing and mailing.

Some consider the use of a corporate purchasing card (p-card) to be outsourcing of some or all of the payment function for those items purchased on the card. Generally it is not looked at this way since the organization using the card still needs to retain some staff, albeit a smaller one, to manage the program and to verify purchases. Since p-cards have become such a large part of the payment landscape, they have been treated separately.

Also, most organizations using p-cards do not consider this to be outsourcing of any responsibility.

CHECK-PRINTING OUTSOURCING

Check printing has numerous potential control issues and problems associated with it. And it definitely falls into the category of non–value-added functions. Hence, some companies choose to outsource their check-printing function, even if they outsource virtually nothing else.

Companies that employ this process for check printing go through their normal check production cycle for everything, except they do not print checks. Instead, they transmit their check issuance file to the outsourcer for printing. In most cases the outsourcer for this service is the company's bank. As long as the proper internal controls are associated with the process, the company is fine, and it avoids a slew of control issues.

OTHER COMMONLY OUTSOURCED ACCOUNTS PAYABLE FUNCTIONS

Meanwhile, a whole slew of other functions that are typically considered part of accounts payable have long been outsourced. A quick list of some of the most common includes:

- Duplicate payment audits
- 1099 issuance
- Unclaimed property compliance
- Telecom audits
- Freight audits
- Sales and use tax compliance

INTERNAL CONTROLS OF THE OUTSOURCER

We can't talk about outsourcing without discussing the subject of ensuring strong internal controls on the part of the outsourcer. For those familiar with the strictures of the Sarbanes-Oxley Act, you know this means a discussion of Statement of Auditing Standards 70, commonly referred to as SAS 70 reports.

Under Sarbanes-Oxley, management is responsible for evaluating the design and effectiveness of the control structure in place both within the third-party provider and between the two organizations if an outsourcer is used and it directly impacts the financial reporting or internal control environment activities. Obviously, if each company were to try to verify the controls of all outsourcers it considered using, the whole process would grind to a gridlocked halt.

The Securities and Exchange Commission (SEC) has provided a solution to this problem. After reviewing Section 404 (the section of Sarbanes-Oxley that addresses internal controls) requirements, the SEC provided a resolution. In June 2004, the SEC announced that companies relying on third-party service providers could rely on Type II SAS 70 reports to assess the internal controls in those operations. Readers should note that SAS 70 was around a long time before Sarbanes-Oxley.

A SAS 70 audit (or *Service Auditor's Examination*, as it is sometimes called) verifies that the control objectives and activities of the subject company are in place. At the end of the examination, assuming that the appropriate controls are in place, a formal report is issued to the service provider. This SAS 70 report, often referred to as the *Service Auditor's Report*, is given to auditors at companies using the services of the outsourcer to permit them to certify the controls of their clients. Basically, there are two types of reports, referred to as Type I and Type II.

Type I Reports

A Type I report includes:

- Independent Service Auditor's Report
- Service organization's description of controls

Several optional features may be included:

- A description of the service auditor's test of operating effectiveness and the results of those tests (this information is provided by the independent service auditor)
- Other information as the service organization chooses to include

This report describes the controls in place at a specific point in time.

In this report the service auditor will offer its opinion on whether the description of its controls presents fairly the relevant aspects of the organization's controls and whether the controls were designed appropriately to achieve the specified control objectives.

Type II Reports

A Type II report includes:

- Independent Service Auditor's Report
- Service organization's description of controls
- A description of the service auditor's test of operating effectiveness and the results of those tests (this information is provided by the independent service auditor)

- Other information that the service organization chooses to provide

The SEC has deemed Type II reports appropriate for companies using third-party service providers to rely on.

This report is not for a specified point in time but rather includes detailed testing of the service organization's controls over a minimum six-month period.

In addition to the items certified in the Type I report, the Type II reports include an opinion as to whether the controls tested were operating with sufficient effectiveness to provide reasonable assurance that control objectives were achieved during the specified period. The important feature to note here is the use of the word *reasonable*. The report does not guarantee that the control objectives have been achieved but rather that there is a reasonable certainty that the objectives have been achieved.

USING THE REPORTS

Organizations that outsource parts of their business process should request SAS 70 Type II reports from their third-party service providers. Of course, this is required only after a determination has been made that the services directly impact financial reporting or internal control environment activities.

However, it is probably a good idea to request these reports even if you are not required to comply with Sarbanes-Oxley. Why? Ask for a SAS 70 Type II report to ensure that the organizations that are being used to handle outsourced functions are employing strong internal controls. You will get good information regarding the outsourcer's controls and effectiveness of those controls.

Be aware that many professionals are critical of SAS reports because they are not as stringent as the Sarbanes-Oxley Act itself. They do, however, provide a guidepost to some level of control. And they can be requested by any organization, regardless of whether it is public or not.

The fact that the organization has gone to the trouble and expense of getting the SAS reports is a good sign that it takes controls seriously. While it is not a guarantee, it is the best indication available today.

REFERENCES

Without a doubt, ask all potential outsourcers for references and then check them out. Like anything else, it is unlikely that the outsourcer will provide a reference that will not give a favorable report. So they should be taken with a grain of salt.

If your accounts payable manager belongs to any professional group or goes to accounts payable conferences, have him or her ask peers if any have had experience with the outsourcer. Unsolicited testimonials are the best, although they are often difficult to find.

Finally, when checking a reference, ask for the references they were given when they initially started doing business with the outsourcer. Check back with those organizations. They will have been doing business with the particular outsourcer for some time and should be able to tell you if the outsourcer stands up over the long haul.

BETA SITES

The payment market is an interesting place right now. Outsourcing and automated products are in their infancy. Many new offerings are coming to market every month. While few like to be one of the first onboard, there is a small group of professionals who like to be on the bleeding edge. Whether you are considering outsourcing (or looking at an automated product), you may have an opportunity to keep your costs lower or at nothing, if you are willing to be a beta site for one of these offerings. A beta site gives the supplier the opportunity to try out its product on a live site while getting feedback from the end user. The product developer likes beta tests as it lets them get real-life data into their product to iron out any kinks. But what's in it for the end user?

By participating as a beta site, you often get the opportunity to put your two cents in and have the developer create features that are to your liking and might meet special requirements of your company or industry. Plus, you should be offered this opportunity at either a reduced cost or perhaps for free for a year or two.

If your organization is a household name, you will be considered a prime candidate for beta testing. This is because once the product goes live, the developer will be able to list you as a user. Thus, you may be able to negotiate a better deal: either lower cost or a longer free period. Use of your name on the client list should be discussed up front.

Keep in mind that use of the product during the beta phase will result in more work for your employees. Some won't mind, as they like to be involved with new developments, but others will complain loudly and bitterly about the extra work. And no matter what the developer tells you, it will mean extra work. It can be a lot of fun and an exhilarating experience for the professionals willing to work with the developer, but it will take up extra time.

Finding beta opportunities is not always easy. Sometimes you will be approached. These opportunities are rarely posted. Your accounts payable manager may hear of them at trade shows or through a network of peers. Occasionally the developer will approach a trade publisher asking for recommendations. If you are at all interested, make sure that fact is well known.

CONVERGENCE FACTOR

In the last few years, another issue has emerged. Several companies have begun to develop electronic invoicing products. They are similar in many ways but all have their own little nuances. However, if you take a step back and look at how these products operate and compare those processes with the way outsourcers perform their tasks, a very interesting vision emerges.

There is very little difference between some of these electronic invoicing products and the actual outsourcing of invoice processing. It is simply a matter of nomenclature. Many electronic invoicing products on the market today are simply the outsourcing of the invoice processing function, albeit under a more acceptable name.

The end of the process results in a payment file being created. This either can be returned to the paying organization for the printing and mailing of checks, or it can be sent to a bank to perform those tasks. This file can also contain information about payments to be initiated via the automated clearing house (ACH), p-cards, or wire transfer, although to be honest, to date, very little p-card activity is initiated this way.

As mentioned, p-cards are generally not considered outsourcing. Yet if you take a look at the net effect on the payment process, you might very well conclude that use of p-cards represents some level of outsourcing. This is just another example of the blurring lines between outsourcing and use of third-party products.

OUTSOURCING VERSUS AUTOMATION

Some of the products on the market might not represent a complete outsourcing of the function but rather an automation of the process. The result is a process that requires fewer employees and is typically more efficient, eliminating human keying errors and permitting one employee to handle the workload of several.

The politically acceptable explanation for the adoption of these products (as well as for outsourcing, in general) is that it will free employees to handle more productive, value-added work. That fact, by itself, may be true. But it is not what happens in most cases.

Whether turning to outsourcing or to an automated process, organizations are looking to cut costs. In many cases the biggest expense is headcount. Reducing it is also the easiest way to cost-justify a new process.

IS IT OUTSOURCING OR NOT?

Senior executives at most organizations do not care whether the approach taken is outsourcing or not. Whether it is an automated approach or a complete outsourcing is irrelevant. They have bottom-line responsibility, and as long as internal controls are maintained and state and federal laws are not broken, they are indifferent to how a task is performed as long as the cost is kept down.

Thus savvy service providers are developing products that are essentially outsourcing, but often do not go by that name. Instead, they are cloaked behind a politically acceptable name, and everyone is happy—everyone, that is, except the employees who ultimately lose their jobs.

IMPLICATIONS

Organizations

Organizations outsource to save money. When all the talk of process improvements and focusing on core competency has been cleared through, almost without exception, the real reason for pursing an outsourcing alternative is cost reduction.

An organization could not function for very long without someone paying close attention to the payment function, but it is definitely a support function and, from a profit and loss standpoint, a cost center. With few exceptions, it does not bring revenue into an organization.

While use of an outsourcing alternative for support functions does allow that organization to focus on its core competencies and take advantage of best practices, without the cost savings, few would pursue the outsourced approach. Thus, the payment function is one that some consider outsourcing. The flip side of the coin is that many organizations are not willing to give up control of their money, and that is what they see when the issue of outsourcing payments is raised. Hence the relative popularity of products that effectively minimize the number of people needed to handle the process without calling the change *outsourcing*.

Personnel

The expense saving associated with outsourcing or the purchase of a new automated process is typically measured in reduced head-count. It's that simple. Other metrics are hard to quantify and often subjective.

If you are a professional whose career is dependent on payment processes, it is critical that you recognize these trends. The hand-writing is on the wall. Regardless of whether you like it or not, outsourcing and/or automation of big chunks of the function are likely to invade your professional payment domain in one form or another. But this does not have to mean the end of your career.

Recognize the trend and get ahead of it. By no means will this mean the end of the accounts payable function. However, it does imply that the function will change radically over the next few years. What you do with this information is up to you.

Do nothing and your chances of being on the list of those considered redundant when the processes are adopted are great.

However, if you decide to take charge of the change, the odds are much better that you will be a career survivor driving change within the organization, managing it, and helping your organization improve the efficiency and profitability of the payment function.

The decision is yours. The functionality is already starting to change, and the transformation will only pick up speed in the next few years. You can either drive that bus or be driven over by the bus. The choice is up to you.

Payment Trend

There will be continued growth in the market for payment outsourcing (and automation). Learn all you can about it and find ways to efficiently integrate those pieces that work into your organization's payment process.

16

CHECK FRAUD: PREVENTION TOOLS AND TECHNIQUES

INTRODUCTION

Check fraud is a serious problem. It is everyone's responsibility to prevent it. According to the experts, about 10 years ago, it was among the fastest-growing industries in the United States—and they weren't joking. Chapter 14 discussed how to prevent duplicate payments. Those techniques are important when it comes to fraud as well. Very roughly speaking, the same controls that protect an organization from making a duplicate payment will also help guard against fraud.

HISTORY

Once upon a time, when corporate life was certainly simpler, banks routinely ate the losses associated with check fraud. But those losses grew to the point where that stance was no longer feasible or reasonable, at least from the banks' point of view. In 1990, the Uniform Commercial Code (UCC) was changed, and the concepts of ordinary care and comparative negligence were introduced. These concepts are used to determine liability if there is a check fraud. With check fraud continuing to rocket, every organization needs to full understand their responsibilities.

The check fraud problem is substantially larger than it was in 1993—and remember, that was after the banks had had enough and the UCC was changed. According to figures from the 2003 Nilson Report, check fraud exceeded $20 billion per year. This is a significant increase from the $5 billion figure reported in 1993 and from 1996, when it was $12 billion. Looking at these numbers, it's easy to understand why banks have had enough and companies are taking aggressive steps to protect themselves.

Not only has the check fraud problem exploded, but the resulting changes in the UCC have had an unintended consequence. While the goal was to reduce check fraud, the result of the change was to put corporations and their bankers on opposite sides of the table. Let's face it, if there's a loss, someone has to pay for it. And with banks no longer willing to foot the bill, the issue can get ugly. There have been more than a few instances where a bank and a large corporate client parted ways when the bank refused to eat check fraud losses that resulted from the corporate client's negligence.

THE LAW

There are three parties to be considered when assessing responsibility for a check fraud loss:

1. The party that issued the check (that's your company)
2. The bank of first deposit
3. The collecting bank

The idea is that each party operates in a manner that minimizes the possibility for check fraud. In Articles 3 and 4, the UCC describes the responsibilities needed under the concepts of ordinary care and comparative negligence. Generally speaking, the losses associated with a check fraud are allocated to the parties (just listed) sharing the responsibility for the prevention of the check fraud. The allocation depends on the parties' ability to prevent the fraud. In other words, it depends on the amount of contributory negligence assessed to each party. In these discussions, you will hear constant reference to contributory negligence.

The other contributing factor is a concept called ordinary care. This requires that customers follow "reasonable commercial standards" for their industry or business. This seemingly innocuous statement can have significant ramifications, so don't overlook it. An organization's failure to exercise ordinary care will be considered to have substantially contributed to the fraud. Or to put it another way, the organization is considered to have neglected its obligation to exercise ordinary care.

IMPACT

What is meant by "ordinary care" when it comes to your disbursement practices? Now, if you are thinking that reasonable care means good strong internal controls related to your check preparation and storage processes, you are on the right track. But that's only part of your responsibilities.

Your banker will probably consider that organizations that do not use positive pay are not exercising ordinary care. In fact, you may be asked to sign a letter indicating that the bank offered you a positive pay product but you declined to use it. Be aware that if you sign this letter—and your bank may insist you either sign it or begin using positive pay—you may have signed away all your protections.

Without a doubt, positive pay is one of the best steps a company can take to stop check fraud in its tracks. Every company should use it. But a number of organizations still do not.

Some banks are so insistent that their customers use positive pay that they insert a statement in their deposit agreements that effectively places the liability for check fraud on their customers if they do not use positive pay. Typically the treasurer or controller will handle this document. If they are not sufficiently informed about the positive pay issue, this could slip past them.

You may be wondering if inclusion of such a statement is legal. The UCC does not permit banks simply to disclaim their responsibility. However, the rules do not prevent parties from agreeing to shift liability from one to another. And that is exactly what your company has done if it accepts that depository agreement.

BEST POSITIVE PAY PRACTICE

First, it is strongly advocated that you use positive pay. It is simply the best safeguard your company has against check fraud. See the discussion that follows for an explanation of positive pay and the enhancements that some banks have introduced to make the product stronger.

If your organization is not using positive pay, ask to see the deposit agreement to make sure that the bank has not passed the liability to your organization. Claiming ignorance will get you nowhere if a fraudulent check makes it through the system. Even if there is nothing in the deposit agreement, you might ask the treasurer, controller, or whoever is responsible for banking relationships if the firm ever signed a letter refusing to accept positive pay. Some banks require this and use it as a defense to shift payment responsibility to their customers in cases of check fraud. We've heard of several cases where the bank refused an account if positive pay wasn't used without a signed letter.

Check fraud is a fact of business life. No matter how careful an organization is, it happens. Virtually every company gets hit at one point or another. By knowing what the risks and alternatives are, you will be in the best position to limit your firm's exposure in case of check fraud.

POSITIVE PAY AND ITS COUSINS

Virtually every check expert agrees that positive pay is a product banks use to help thwart check fraud. However, crooks are a resourceful lot. Just as quickly as the legitimate business world develops protection against them, fraudsters find ways to circumvent the safeguards. This has happened to some extent with positive pay and has led to some very interesting innovations as the corporate world protects itself against check fraud.

Basic Model

The basic positive pay model requires that a company send a file to the bank each time it does a check run. The file contains check numbers and dollar amounts of all checks issued. The bank then matches all checks that come in for clearing against this file. Once a check comes in and is paid, the item is removed from the file and cannot be paid again.

This approach took a big whack at the check fraud problem. It eliminated several huge check fraud issues including:

- The copying of one check numerous times and the subsequent cashing of all of them
- The altering of the dollar amount on a check
- The complete manufacture of fraudulent checks drawn on an organization's bank account

What the basic model did not address were checks cashed by tellers and checks where the payee's name was changed. Additionally, companies that could not produce a check-issued file for transmission to their banks were left unprotected. And, as might be expected, once the crooks got wind of positive pay, some adjusted their sights, focusing more on changing the payee's name rather than the dollar amount and on checks cashed at teller windows. But before we look at the products that address those issues, let's take a look at the banks' response for those companies that could not produce a check-issued file.

Reverse Positive Pay

Recognizing that not every organization was able or willing to produce the tape needed for positive pay, banks introduced another service. It's called reverse because it reverses the process. Each morning the bank tells the company what checks have been presented for clearing. It is up to the company to check those listings and make sure that they are all legitimate. Typically, there is a fall-back position if the company does not notify the bank; usually that is that the bank pays on the check. The action should be discussed with the bank when the reverse positive pay relationship is initially set up.

Teller Positive Pay

Once it became obvious that checks were being verified before they were honored, crooks realized that most tellers did not have this information and started cashing phony checks in person. Some banks now make this information available to their tellers on the platforms. If your bank does so, ask how frequently this information is updated. Some update continuously while others only update this information overnight. If it is only overnight, you could have some angry or annoyed vendors or employees on your hands if they try to cash checks you give them on the same day they are issued. A phone call usually takes care of these situations.

Payee Name Positive Pay

Recognizing that fraudsters were reduced to focusing their efforts on changing payee names on checks, a few banks have taken up the fight in that regard. In addition to the check number and dollar amount, they will also verify the payee name.

Will this completely stop check fraud? Probably not, but it certainly will make it more difficult for the crooks trying to separate your company from its funds.

YOUR CHECKS

It is the responsibility of the organization issuing checks to make them difficult to copy. Check stock should have security features built into them. Most experts agree that incorporating three features into the checks is considered to be exercising reasonable care. These security features are just some that can be incorporated into checks:

- American Bankers Association (ABA) check endorsement clause
- Anti-splice backer
- Copy void endorsement
- Copy void in check pantograph
- Covert fluorescent fibers
- Endorsement warning
- Fourdriner true watermark
- Gradient two-color blend pantograph
- Image-friendly amount box
- Fluorescent fibers
- Control numbers
- Microprinting
- Multi language chemical void
- Non negotiable stub backer
- Overt fibers
- Padlock security
- Simulated watermark
- Solvent-reactive color spotting
- Thermochromic ink
- Toner adhesion enhancement
- Voidless postal window
- Warning band
- Watermark certification seal

Readers should be aware that there have been reports that the VOID pantograph does not work with some of the newer copy machines.

Do not take a shortcut in this arena by trying to save a few cents by purchasing the cheapest checks available.

CARE OF CHECK STOCK

It is also your responsibility, especially if you use preprinted check stock, that you not make it easy for someone to steal some of your check stock. This means keeping the stock in a secure location with limited availability.

It also means that as checks are produced, signed, and mailed, they be watched carefully. Leaving checks sitting unattended in the mailroom makes it easy for anyone who casually strolls through to pick off a few. Thus, it is generally recommended that checks be delivered to the mailroom right before they are to be taken to be mailed. Otherwise, they should remain locked away.

This brings up the delicate issue of how checks are handled if manual signatures need to be added after the check production process. It is not unusual to go into an executive's empty office and see a folder of checks sitting out on the desk awaiting signature, or half signed. This is not good. Again, it would not be difficult for a thief to pick up a check or two and stroll off.

Common sense will dictate how your check stock and checks awaiting mailing are handled. Don't make it easy for someone to swipe one of your checks.

OTHER CHECK SAFETY ISSUES

When it comes to check stock, there is one other issue to consider. Some organizations keep a small checkbook for emergency payments. That checkbook might be kept in a file cabinet or someone's desk. It may or may not be locked, and many people may have access to the file—usually for other purposes. If you have such a checkbook, evaluate whether you really need it. If the decision is affirmative, consider how it is stored, who has access to it, and whether some of that be changed.

Along the same lines, if you use a laser printer to produce checks, incorporate appropriate passwords and user IDs to ensure that only authorized people are able to print checks. Under no circumstances allow the sharing of passwords. This is such a serious breach in security that some organizations consider it a firing offense. Do not allow overworked managers to give their passwords to underlings just to get the checks issued on a busy day. An employee intent on stealing will remember those codes.

If you use safety paper and have your laser printer print all pertinent information on your checks, still keep the paper under lock and key and account for all sheets. While safety paper is not as valuable to a thief as preprinted check stock, it still has some value. Plus, your controls in this area demonstrate that you are exercising ordinary care.

RECONCILIATION

The changes in the UCC require prompt bank statement reconciliation in order to avoid responsibility for fraudulent checks. From a strong internal control standpoint, it is also a good idea to reconcile quickly. Make this a top priority for the professional responsible for this task.

Given that there may be times when other work requirements make it difficult to get these reconciliations done, here are a few helpful techniques to detect obvious forgeries:

- Fan through a group of returned checks. A counterfeit may stand out as having a slightly different color from the rest of the checks in the batch.
- The perforations, or lack thereof, may also give a counterfeit note away. Most checks produced by legitimate printers

are perforated and have at least one rough edge. Those created by fraudsters generally do not have such imperfections. This once hard-and-fast rule must be used with some care. The checks generated by in-house laser printers, for example, tend to have microperforations that are more difficult to detect.

SEGREGATION OF DUTIES

Duties within the organization should be segregated so that no one is in a position to issue a fraudulent check. Some of the duties that should be segregated follow.

- The person responsible for bank reconciliation should not:
  - Handle unclaimed property reporting
  - Be a signer on a bank account
- The person who is a check signer should not:
  - Authorize an invoice for payment on an account that he or she is also a signer
  - Have ready access to the check stock
- A person who is responsible for the check stock should not:
  - Be an authorized signer
  - Handle the bank reconciliations
- The person who is responsible for the master vendor file should not:
  - Be an authorized signer
  - Be able to approve invoices for payment
  - Handle unclaimed property
- The person responsible for unclaimed property should not
  - Have responsibility for bank reconciliation

- ○ Have access to the master vendor file

You may be able to come up with others.

MASTER VENDOR FILE AND CHECK FRAUD

The master vendor file is one of the most overlooked functions when it comes to payments. Even fewer think of it when the topic of check fraud is raised. However, by carefully manipulating the master vendor file, one of your employees could have a check diverted to him or her. Here's one simple scenario.

Let's say you have a large vendor called IBM. Your employee opens up a bank account for a company called Independent Bakers Machines. He then puts an address change in the Remit To field in your master vendor file right before a large payment is due. IBM's invoice is processed through your regular channels and then mailed to the altered Remit To address. (If your employee has half a brain, he did not have that payment go to his home address but rather to a PO Box.) Once the check is received and cashed, the address in the master vendor file is changed back to the correct one. If strict controls and reporting are not kept on the file, you will be hard pressed to prevent this fraud or to catch it.

The example given here is a simple one. Crooks who are smarter and more devious than I could cook up even more. Many controls and best practices should be employed around the master vendor file. They are covered in depth in accounts payable books. For the purpose of this discussion, these are important:

- Limit the ability to add or change information in the master vendor file to no more than three individuals.
- Produce a weekly report of all changes made to the master vendor file and have it reviewed by a senior-level executive.

- Require a submitter and an authorizer for any additions or changes made to the master vendor file. Do not enter a change on the basis of one individual's request.

Payment Trends

Check fraud is a fact of corporate life. It is here to stay. Crooks have no heart—they'll steal wherever they can. It does not matter if your organization is large or small, for profit or not for profit; everyone is a target. There is no such thing as being too small to steal from. As new approaches are developed to fight check fraud, crooks will find ways around them. Thus, it is imperative that all organizations keep up to date on all the latest check-fraud-fighting products as they are developed.

17

ACH Fraud: Prevention Tools and Techniques

INTRODUCTION

Everyone should read this chapter—regardless of whether you make electronic payments or not. The reason is simple. Anyone with a bank account can be victimized by automated clearing house (ACH) fraud if they do not take the appropriate steps to guard themselves. Don't be lulled into a false sense of security because you do not make ACH payments.

Payment fraud via the ACH, while it is not nearly as large a problem as check fraud, is a serious issue. Savvy payment professionals understand that they must take care to ensure their companies are not victimized by crooks who know their way around computers and the banking system. Aiding in that effort, banks and several service providers are now working to develop products to help thwart this type of crime. What follows is a roundup of the products on the market and coming to market. It is expected that this market will become more robust and additional products will be added over time. If your bank is not among those discussed here, do not assume it does not have ACH fraud protection products. Ask.

ACH BLOCKS

ACH blocks are the simplest of all the products to use. They allow companies to notify their banks that ACH debits should not be allowed on certain accounts. With a block in place, no ACH debit, even one that is authorized, will be able to get through on a given account.

Organizations are advised to put blocks in place on all accounts where ACH activity is not likely to be used. Readers using this handy tool are advised to keep track of which accounts they have put blocks on. Otherwise, they could end up with egg on their face when a vendor is given authorization to use an ACH debit and everyone has forgotten that the block was put on the account a year or two earlier.

For some time this was the only tool available to block unauthorized ACH transactions, and many organizations put them on all accounts. Many companies put ACH blocks on all accounts but one, thus enabling them to accommodate a few vendors (or taxing authorities) that insisted on using an ACH debit.

If your organization was one of those that put blocks on numerous accounts, you should periodically review which accounts have blocks on them to determine whether those blocks still make sense.

ACH FILTERS

An ACH filter allows organizations to give their banks a list of companies authorized to debit their accounts. The banks will then "filter" incoming debits and allow through only those that are on the list submitted earlier. This filter does not check for dollar amounts or whether the particular transaction has been authorized, only that the company doing the debiting is on the approved list.

Readers should be aware that this product is sometimes referred to as ACH positive pay, although in this writer's mind that is not the correct appellation. The line is blurred even further because some banks match the identities of those attempting to debit an account with those on the list provided by the company, and exceptions are reported to the customer to review before payment. Only authorized electronic transactions are allowed to be withdrawn from your account.

ACH POSITIVE PAY

A robust positive pay product for the ACH environment is not universally available today, but it is on its way. A number of banks were surveyed about this issue, and this is what was found. Clearly, the list is only a sampling of what is available. As you will see, with the exception of the first listing, the products are basically blocks and filters.

- *LaSalle National Bank* has an online service that allows you to manage your ACH origination file schedules, search and view transaction data, receive automated notification, and input control totals. You can view all incoming debits attempting to post to your account on a daily basis. You can either accept or return each item. You can place an authorization record on LaSalle's system for any ACH debit you accept. The service will filter incoming transactions by matching against your authorizations.
- *Commerce Bank* offers several levels of debit-receipt screening and blocks. "Unlike Positive Pay, we do not receive regular issue files' for ACH payments," says Tom Gregory of Commerce. Alternatively, Commerce allows its customers

to disallow debits at the account level and at the originator ID level. It also encourages commercial customers to isolate debits into discrete accounts and inspect those accounts on a daily basis, allowing time to identify suspects and instruct the bank to return items.

In anticipation of National Automated Clearing House Association (NACHA) rules changes to allow business check conversion to ACH, the bank is integrating ACH payments into the Positive Pay presentment/match process.

- *Bank of America's* fraud protection feature focuses on ACH blocks and filters. These authorize the bank to block and return all unauthorized ACH transactions, or send the bank IDs for trading partners who are authorized to send ACH activity.
- *Huntington Bank* will send daily ACH activity alerts to its customers who request such information.
- *Wells Fargo* offers what it calls "ACH Fraud Filter." It offers protection against unauthorized ACH transactions, with both stop and review options. This allows organizations to stop and return unauthorized ACH transactions; pay or return transactions presented for review; preauthorize certain transactions to be paid; and view detailed and summary transaction reports.

WHO'S OFFERING WHAT TODAY

CheckFree

"We do have a product line for ACH Positive Pay," explains CheckFree's David Redman, director of ACH Global Treasuries Sales Support. "It works as an add-on module to our mainframe ACH application called PEP+. We market this product as the Electronic Payments Authorizations (EPA). The module basically allows for the financial institutions to designate authorization records at the account level."

If this functionality is turned on, only those items that have authorizations set up will be allowed to process through the financial institution's system. If an authorization is not set up, the item rejects and the financial institution's customer is notified. Should the end customer wish to allow the transaction to process, then that customer would need to set up an authorization record that same day because the item will "recollect" the next morning. If the authorization has been added, then the item processes normally. If there is still no authorization, the item rejects back to the originator.

Bottom-line Technologies

In most cases it is the bank that provides these services to corporate customers, says Bottomline's Strategic Project executive, Michael A. Vigue. A service such as this requires two elements: the interface through which the client will decision suspect debits and maintain debit rules and the back-office system that imposes the debit block on incoming debit requests.

"The back-office system in use at most larger banks is provided by CheckFree and available with their platinum upgrade to Pep+. The module is called Exchange. Exchange comes with a tool set that can be used to deploy the client interface. The challenge that banks have with this approach to an interface is that they want some integration into their existing online cash management applications. In addition, a lot of the banks just don't want to spend the time developing the interface. As such, Bottomline has developed a new module in our online Global Payments platform that provides the client interface for the suspect decisioning and rules maintenance of ACH Positive Pay items. Our interface currently works only with CheckFree's Pep + system," explains Vigue.

Bottomline is currently testing this product with one of the nation's largest financial holding companies operating a large banking network in the upper Midwest and Mid-Atlantic regions.

DEMAND DRAFT FRAUD

Demand draft fraud is so mind bogglingly easy, it's not hard to see why crooks are so attracted to it. In fact, we wonder why it hasn't become more popular with those who'd rather spend their time filching your money than earning it honestly. What follows is an in-depth look at demand draft fraud, how it is executed, what your obligations are under the law, and what you can do to protect your company.

What Demand Drafts Are

If you're scratching your head wondering what demand drafts are, you are not alone. This little-known payment device was designed to accommodate legitimate telemarketers who receive authorization from consumers to take money out of the consumer's checking account. This payment alternative is very similar to writing a check—except that it requires no signature.

In place of the authorized signature on the check, "signature not required," "your depositor has authorized this payment to payee," or similar wording is used. Since the check processing areas at banks are completely automated, the signature line is virtually never checked.

In the telemarketer example, this is a creative payment approach that enables the transaction to proceed smoothly. Demand drafts are also sometimes referred to as remotely created checks.

You can see there is potential for check fraud in this arrangement; but any time a check is used for payment, there is also the possibility for abuse. Once the thief has the account number and the name of the account owner, check fraud is merely a matter of conscience, opportunity, and a few dollars for technology.

Demand Drafts and Qchex.com

For a short time, an outfit called Qchex.com dramatically lowered the bar for entry for those wishing to commit payment fraud. No longer was it necessary to have those few dollars for technology. It wasn't even necessary to know the name of the account holder—only the account number and the routing code.

The frauds committed by people using the Qchex.com product were so massive, the company was forced to shut down. With Qchex, the task of creating a fraudulent check had become even easier and the results have been ugly. How bad is the problem? One institution involved indicates that over 70% (yes, 70%) of the demand drafts it encounters are fraudulent. And *that* is a serious problem.

It should be noted that the company wasn't committing the fraud; it simply offered a product with so few controls that crooks in droves took advantage of it.

Demand Draft Responsibilities

The problem has gotten so out of hand that the Federal Reserve is considering a proposal to set a new standard that would put the liability for fraudulent drafts on the bank that cashes the draft in the first place. This would place the responsibility to authenticate the draft with that institution. It will be interesting to see how the banks react to this proposal. It would also add some additional protections. The paying bank would have 60 days to return bad checks and consumers' rights would be spelled out.

A few opponents have even suggested banning demand drafts, but that does not seem likely.

Protecting against Demand Draft Fraud

Companies can do a number of things to protect themselves against demand draft fraud.

- Be careful with your bank account numbers. Do not give them out unless there is a good reason.
- Keep bank account information in a secure location and give it only to employees who need the data. Do not keep a list of all bank accounts lying on your desk where anyone who comes by can see it.
- Use positive pay.
- Reconcile your bank statements in a very timely manner.
- Consider increasing the use of purchase cards (p-cards) and ACH payments
- Don't automatically deposit every small-dollar check that comes in the door. Some crooks send small-dollar checks as a means of getting the company's bank account information. It shows up on the back of deposited checks.
- Reconcile all incoming checks and deposit only those from companies with which you have an ongoing business relationship.
- Use different bank accounts for deposit activity and payments. Then, if crooks do get bank information from the back of a small-dollar check, they won't be able to use it and you'll have the last laugh. They'll have given your firm a few dollars and gotten useless information for it in return.

PAYMENT TREND

It is unlikely that crooks will ignore the "opportunities" for electronic payment fraud for long. It is important that all organizations, whether they use electronic payments or not, take the appropriate steps to protect against it.

18

CONCLUDING THOUGHTS

INTRODUCTION

By now your head is probably spinning. The old notion of getting an invoice and simply writing a check should have vanished from your thought process. It's a new world out there when it comes to payments. This chapter has a few bits of concluding advice to help you fine-tune your payments process and make it more efficient.

SELECTING THE BEST TOOL

What payment tool will be used to pay the invoice will depend on what you've selected as the right tool for the vendor in question. It will also depend on the dollar limitations you may have placed on the tool. This last issue is an important consideration when trying to grow a purchase card (p-card) program. If the limits are too low, it will be difficult to grow the program.

Repetitive transactions, if they are the same time each time period for the same dollar amount, can be set up in advance to happen automatically. The wire transfer mechanism and automated clearing house (ACH) work well for this type of expenditure. Similarly, many programs permit organizations to set these up to be to included automatically in certain check runs. Repetitive transactions should be checked periodically to ensure that they still make sense. More than one organization has ended up with egg on its face when it discovered it was still making lease payments on equipment it no longer owned or mortgage payments on a property sold months earlier.

Small-dollar purchases are ideal for p-cards, if the organization has them and if the vendor accepts them. If either of those conditions fails to exist, the purchases should be paid for with an ACH. To be perfectly honest, it makes little financial sense to process a $15 invoice, although the obligation must be met. Alternatives include having an employee pay for the item and requesting reimbursement through the travel and entertainment process or the petty cash box.

Multiple small-dollar expenditures with the same vendor can be handled in a number of ways. Of course, p-cards can be used, especially by organizations looking to increase their volume in that area. Alternatively, consider making an exception to the never-pay-from-statements rule. These vendors can be designated as "only pay from statement" vendors. Then once a month, take the statement and pay the total amount, after verifying, of course, that all transactions are legitimate. This approach is ideal for overnight delivery services, messenger services, and temporary help. But do take care to verify that all transactions are legitimate and belong to your organization. One duplicate payment vendor reported recovering over $1 million for a large client when another's charges were included on statements.

Large-dollar transactions can be paid using any of the payment tools discussed. Dollar limits on p-cards may prevent that from being a viable tool. It goes without saying that large-dollar transactions should not be paid out of the petty cash box.

NETTING

Often two companies will have a symbiotic relationships, both selling and buying from each other. In these cases, it might appear that the simplest payment approach would be to net payments, having only one party making a smaller payment to the other. Many companies involved in such relationships do just that.

However, from a tracking standpoint as well as ease of checking on payment status, this is less than ideal unless the audit trail associated with both transactions is impeccable. This situation rarely occurs. It is recommended that each party pay the other in its entirety for whatever is owed. While this can lead to confrontations if one party is a tardy payer, it generally is much simpler on other fronts.

CREDITS

An issue similar to that of netting is the subject of outstanding credits. Often the organization that is entitled to credits does not find out about their existence for many months. Why this happens is the subject for a different forum. The focus here is the payment function and how to treat these credits once they are uncovered.

Ideally, again to keep the audit trail clean, the preferred way to treat them is to request a check from vendors. Some vendors refuse to make payments for credits. You can usually get a vendor to cut a check for the credit, but often you'll have to make an issue out of it, and many people prefer to avoid this if at all possible.

The alternative is to take the credit against an open invoice, paying less than what is shown on the invoice. If you do this, communicate it to the vendor, include the details on the remittance advice, and keep very good records yourself. Otherwise you will find the vendor indicating that you short paid the invoice. That's just part of the reason that requesting a separate payment is the preferred choice of action.

MAKING YOUR PAYMENT PROCESS MOST EFFICIENT

The goal of this book is to provide guidelines for the new payment vehicles that are available to organizations. Along the way it is important not to lose sight of the fact that the real goal is simply to make the payment process more efficient and as cost effective as possible. The list that follows provides some guidelines to help with that.

- *Don't adopt a new payment approach simply because it is there.* Evaluate first if it will work in your shop. Just because it worked at the company down the street doesn't mean it will work for your company shop. Adopt processes because they will enhance current operations, not simply because they are new. Along the same lines, don't reject a new process simply because it is new. While you may not always want to be the first kid on the block when it comes to a new process, there's nothing wrong with being the second or third.
- *Don't allow antiquated views to hamper the payment process.* Continually challenge old notions that "this would never work in our organization."
- *Get rid of as much paper as possible.* This means finding ways to get rid of those terribly inefficient, cost-intensive paper checks, and paper invoices as well.
- *Minimize, if not eliminate, any inefficient processes.* Start with petty cash. It is extremely time consuming, inefficient, and the easiest way to open the door to fraud. Look for processes that address a low volume number of payments. When you have identified those processes, evaluate whether the process is efficient and whether you should drive payment traffic in that direction. If that is not the case, look for ways to handle those payments differently and eliminate the process.
- *Eliminate rekeying.* Doing this usually means moving to some sort of electronic invoicing: either electronic data

interchange (EDI) or e-invoicing service. (This can be a full-blown e-invoicing product or just having invoices delivered electronically in a format that can be easily shared throughout the organization.)

- *Accept the fact that even if your payment volume grows, your staff will not.* In fact, it will likely decrease in size. You can control this to some extent by looking for ways not to replace people when someone leaves. To handle the increased workload, look for products and/or processes that make the operation more efficient.
- *Don't be hesitant to ask for an explanation if you don't understand how something works or what its benefits are.* Similarly, if you even suspect that a rebate or lower cost might be available, ask. All they can say is no.
- *Minimize the occurrence of duplicate payments.* While it is probably not possible to eliminate them completely, it is possible to greatly reduce their number. Of the many things you can do to accomplish this goal, these directly relate to the payment process:
    - Centralize the receipt of invoices.
    - Assign payment type to each vendor.
    - Run duplicate payment checking routines before releasing checks.

WHERE TO GET MORE INFORMATION

Clearly, the options organizations have to make payments are growing. Even existing products are sprouting wings and adding new features and functionality. Consider the case of wire transfers, long considered to be too expensive. Faced with the prospect of losing their wire activity to the less costly ACH, some banks are looking for ways to make wire transfers more cost efficient.

Thus, it is important for the professionals responsible for the payment function to stay on top of the newest developments in this area. Otherwise, they stand the chance of being confronted by their chief financial officer or president who hears about the advance from a peer and wants to know "how come we're not using such and such." What can you do to stay ahead of the payment enhancement curve?

Start with your friendly banker. He or she should provide you with information about the latest enhancements. Now, bankers usually relate information about their products only. That's just one of the reasons most companies have more than one banker. Then, when the banker from Bank A introduces a new product, savvy professionals ask their banker from Bank B if a similar product is being developed. Lacking competitive information, you can turn to the Internet and visit the leading banks' cash management pages to see what new products have been developed recently.

Don't overlook books, newsletters, and, increasingly, electronic newsletters, sometimes called e-zines. These have a wealth of good information.

Conferences on accounts payable, payment matters, treasury issues, and cash management initiatives are another good place to find information. When attending these events, visit vendors' displays and talk to other attendees who may be using some of the products. Your peers are an excellent referral source—both for what's good and what's not working or may have some problems. Even if they are happy with an initiative, don't forget to ask them what they'd do differently if they had to do it again. You can always learn from the problems of others.

Don't overlook the newest educational tool: webinars, also called webcasts, and audio conferences. These allow you to get information doled out in small bits over the Internet and/or phone. Best of all, you can invite the entire staff to hear the lecture for the price of one admission.

Another source of information that is often overlooked by busy professionals: the vendors themselves. Many offer online training or lectures with a product demonstration at the end. Attend as many as you can, especially if there is no charge. You'll learn not only from the educational part of the event but also by watching the product demo. It's an easy way to see a number of vendors without ever leaving your office. If you invite your staff, you'll benefit from their insights as well. Plus, as a side benefit you'll probably improve employee morale.

Payment Trend

Payment products will continue to be developed. Fine-tune yours on a regular basis, taking advantage of those that will enable you to make your process more efficient and less costly. Ignore those that don't, reevaluating those you skipped over from time to time.

ABOUT ACCOUNTS PAYABLE NOW & TOMORROW

Accounts Payable Now & Tomorrow (www.ap-now.com) is a monthly publication devoted to payment issues. Each issue contains:

- Four to six hard-hitting articles offering practical advice on the many problematic issues confronting payables operations everywhere
- Two Guest Columns from the most-respected names in their fields covering specialty functions including: 1099s, sales and use tax, unclaimed property, p-cards, VAT, banking issues (positive pay, ACH, Check 21, etc.), accounting issues (Sarbanes-Oxley, internal controls, etc.), fraud, software and audits, and more
- A Tips, Tactics, and Strategies section . . . and much more

With your paid subscription, you'll also get a weekly e-zine, *e-News from the AP Front*, a quick-read e-mail update, and the opportunity to participate in and get the results from ground-breaking research focused on payment issues.

To receive a sample copy of the print publication, send an e-mail to publisher@ap-now.com with the words "Wiley sent me" in the subject line. Make sure you include your company name, title, and mailing address.

If you would prefer to just be added to the distribution of the complimentary e-zine, simply send the same information with a note to that effect to publisher@ap-now.com.

Accounts Payable Now & Tomorrow is a CRYSTALLUS, Inc. publication. In addition to publishing the newsletter, the firm provides consulting services to organizations looking to reengineer their accounts payable function. It also works in a collaborative nature where we work with existing staff to develop plans for departmental or payment process improvement. Through an alliance, the firm helps those looking for assistance in recovering duplicate payments. Information on these ventures can be obtained by sending an e-mail to publisher@ap-now.com or calling 302-836-0540.

Index